FIND
& KEEP

BECI ORPIN

hardie grant books
MELBOURNE · LONDON

CONTENTS

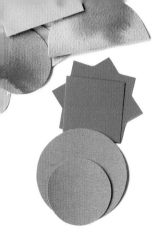

This book is dedicated to my dad Ross and my mum Marg, for teaching me how to be individual, creative and practical all at the same time.

INTRODUCTION

Hello. So, what is this book about? Well, it's my personal take on how to find inspiration and what to do with it – a little trip through my stream of creative consciousness.

"What inspires you?" is probably the question most asked of any creative person. I've come to loathe this question, as not only is it predictable, but I also find it impossible to answer. There are SO MANY things out there that inspire me. And they change on a daily basis.

These days, it's easier than ever to find creative inspiration – especially with the internet at your fingertips. At the risk of sounding ancient, when I was at university there was no internet. But of course, I still managed to find inspiration, as did millions of other creative people before me; I just used the world around me instead of sitting at my computer.

Admittedly, I did have to train myself to do this. In my first year of studying textile design, I used to walk to university. It was a long but pleasant walk, and provided me with excellent headspace. I would think about the assignments I had, and searched the space around me – mental and physical – for ideas to help me complete my projects. To my surprise, it worked. Ideas came from everywhere – window displays, parks or grocery stores – I just had to be looking for them constantly and have my mind open to receive those ideas. Before long, my brain started operating like this automatically, and to this day inspiration comes to me all the time and in many forms.

Getting inspired is only half the fun though. What to do with it – that's the other half! My aim with this book is to not only show you what inspires me, but also what I do with my ideas once I get that flash of inspiration.

I feel infinitely lucky to do what I do. After 15 years or so, it still doesn't feel like a job!

STUDIO

Welcome
to my studio.
Most of my ideas start here. Although
the inspiration for these ideas may have
appeared from elsewhere, the developing,
testing and creating all happens here.

As you will see from the pictures in this chapter
I am a born hoarder, and my studio is always heaving
with books, art supplies, fabrics, paper scraps, old
sketchbooks and a thousand other bits and pieces.
Although it might look like junk to some, all of
these things are important to me. They help
turn the inspiration I find into illustrations,
geometric designs, 3-D objects, clothing
patterns, all sorts of things –
it's a strange sort
of magic!

My studio is in my house. It's the first room you walk into and has a window facing right onto the street, so anyone walking past can see straight in. I always wonder what people think when they peer in (and they usually do) and see my messy desk and, more often that not, me, sitting, tapping away on my computer or drawing in my sketchbook.

Sometimes my studio is clean, usually it's not; although it does have some sort of order that makes sense to me. My studio doesn't even have a door to separate it from the rest of my house, so it's often filled with mewing cats, yelling children or visiting friends. Unsurprisingly, late at night is my favourite studio time, when it's quiet and peaceful.

My studio is reflective of the boundary-less work/life situation I choose to live in. It may not be exactly perfect, but it does keep me very satisfied, and provides the best creative haven I could ever hope for. It also enables me to work across many mediums – digital, collage, screen-printing, drawing, painting, sculpture, just to name a few. I think the more mediums you use, the more you learn about your own creativity, and the more you can explore design elements such as colour, shape and form.

COLOUR

I am fanatical about colour. I will labour over it for hours – testing with paints, pencils and on my computer, too. I love how colour can change the mood of something in an instant. With my personal work, I tend to have a favourite set of colours, which slowly evolves over time.

The artwork below is something of a constant work in progress. It originally grew from an idea I had developed for a group exhibition piece, and I was developing it further for a magazine called *Art Park*. I drew up the marbled pattern on my computer and liked how it had a cosmic look when combined with other floating shapes and the girl. I was favouring pastel colours at the time, with a few unexpected pops of brighter coral for interest. The colours seemed to suit this illustration and its other-worldly theme. It kept it quite feminine as well.

Once I was happy with this artwork, I started playing around with the colours in paint in my sketchbook, trying to see if I could further develop the same palette and find something else to apply it to.

At the same time I was also working on a collaboration with one of my textile design idols, Rae Ganim. Rae had run an amazing textile company for 30 years and had recently opened her own shop, Ganim, in Melbourne. Together, we designed these mushroom canisters. Rae found a company to make them and I designed and painted faces and patterns onto each one. Even though it was a commercial venture it was still a very personal project for me, as each mushroom was produced in limited numbers. We decided if they were successful (they were!) we would change the colours for each series, so it seemed the perfect opportunity to use the colour palette I had developed earlier in my sketchbook.

MUSHROOMS

We wanted the mushrooms to remain neutral with splashes of colour, so the wood would remain the hero and we wouldn't lose their 'crafted' feel. The colours suited the simple geometric shapes and helped make the faces look sweet but not over-the-top cute.

SHAPE

As you can probably tell, I have a thing for geometric shapes. I'm not sure what it is – maybe it's their simplicity, or perhaps it's childhood nostalgia. Regardless of where this love comes from, these shapes have been popping up in my work for a long time. So, when it came to designing a new print for a market stall I had coming up, I decided to use a geometric design.

In my studio I have a tiny A5 screen printer called a gocco printer. They are from Japan, but sadly are no longer produced. In the past decade this little printer has seen a revival as designers around the world try to 'save gocco' (Google it!). I think the original inspiration for this print came from a random arrangement of puzzle pieces and a 'surprise ball' that had been sitting on my desk for a few weeks. I had also created some geometric-based collages using similar shapes (see opposite page), and I wanted this work to reflect these designs.

Firstly, I hand-painted my chosen shapes in watercolour, thinking I wanted them to look quite organic. But the more I played around, the more I realised I wanted clean lines, so I redrew each shape with perfect clean-edged lines on my computer.

After much testing, I was finally happy with the shapes and their composition. I mixed ink colours using the puzzle pieces on my desk as a reference. I then launched into printing the final editions for each gocco print.

GOCCO

This is the final print. I was really happy with the way the colours and shapes worked together, combined with the beautiful imperfections that come from gocco printing. It sold out, too!

GRAPHIC

I have been lucky enough to work with the Japanese company GAS As Interface for a few years now. They always approach me with the most amazing opportunities, and this one was definitely my favourite. I was asked (along with five other female artists) to create illustrations for a variety of sweets (cookies, boxed chocolates, jellies etc) for the Japanese department store Isetan. The final designs would appear on the actual sweets, and also on the wrapping and packaging. I started by painting different objects in my sketchbook. I had used the bear face below a few times before in my own products (see opposite page), and loved how it worked with the colour sections. I had also just returned from South Korea with armfuls of coloured paper, so I played around making simple shapes with these too.

On my computer I developed other shapes and images using the same bright colour palette as the bear painting. I had in the back of my mind the whole time, "What would my ultimate sweet look like?" These were getting close. I loved how the patterns and images came together. Even though my final designs were so graphic, they still looked beautiful as sweets and on chocolate boxes.

This, matched with Isetan's addition of fluorescent coral elastic on the box, made them absolutely perfect!

PATTERN

Despite the different mediums I work in, my roots are in textile design, and creating patterns remains my favourite thing to do. When I was asked to design a gift range for Australian clothing chain Sportsgirl, I used one of my all-time favourite influences – folk art. This time, I reinterpreted it in a modern way with clean lines and super-bright colour. I called it 'neon-folk geometry'. I had also just finished a residency at Harvest Textiles (a print company in Melbourne that runs classes and workshops for artists and designers), where I spent a few weeks creating work from coloured paper and screen-printing. I used this work as my starting point. I also really love bears – the guy on the right was hanging in my studio (I think my son Tyke put the ropes around him).

I designed a rain poncho as one of the items in my gift range – perfect for letting loose my neon-folk geometry designs, not to mention the upcoming music festival season!

I started by copying colourful shapes found in folk patterns in my sketchbook.

Production limitations meant I could only have a one-colour print. This was the first print I designed, but I didn't think it was fun enough.

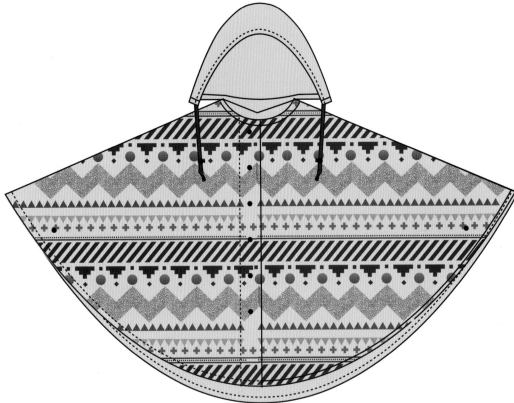

PONCHO

So I went back to the drawing board, using similar shapes, but adding some figurative elements such as the bear, and making the repeating pattern a bit more complex.

With a final addition of fluorescent pink, my neon-folk geometry design was complete, and the poncho was looking good enough to rock at any festival.

STUDIO
PROJECTS

So, now
that you've had a
sneak peek at some of the things I
make in my studio, here are some
projects you can make in your own
studio. If you don't have the luxury
of a dedicated creative space, just take
over your lounge room or dining table for
a few hours. I've tried to include projects that
incorporate materials I regularly use in my
studio every day – paper, paint, fabric,
wool etc. And remember, there is no
right or wrong here! As long as you
are enjoying yourself,
you are doing the
right thing.

FUN WITH DYES & BLEACH

{ DIFFICULTY: hard }

During my years as a textile student, I would spend hours in the print room mixing up different-coloured dyes. It's a pretty hard art to master, but using pre-mixed colour dyes at home is much easier and just as much fun. Always check the instructions on your packet of dye when you buy it to see if there's anything else you need, such as salt to set the dye. Beware: dyeing is a messy (and quite often toxic!) business, so make sure you wear old clothes and rubber gloves at all times.

If you'd like a smoother, graduated effect for the pillowcase, move the fabric by smaller increments, such as one-quarter instead of one-third.

YOU WILL NEED

Pillowcase
- plain pale pillowcase
- masking tape
- plastic bag
- elastic band
- dye of your choice
- stainless-steel pot/sink
- rubber gloves
- stick

T-shirt
- plain dark t-shirt
- newspaper/scrap paper
- piece of thick cardboard
- test piece of dark fabric
- bleach
- objects to apply bleach

LET'S GET STARTED

1

PILLOWCASE

Wash and dry the pillowcase if it's brand new, as some fabrics have coatings that prevent dye absorption. Use masking tape to mark a line on the pillowcase indicating where the dye should come to. Use this line as a guide when placing the pillowcase in the dye.

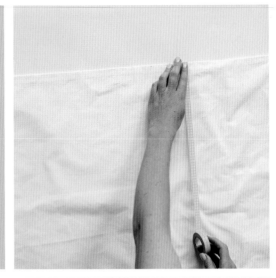

2

Place a plastic bag over the end of the pillowcase that is not being dyed and fasten it with an elastic band. This will protect it from any accidental splashes of dye.

3

Mix up your dye according to the packet instructions in a non-porous vessel (eg stainless-steel pot or sink). The fabric needs to be able to hang over the side of the vessel. Make sure all the dye is dissolved to avoid inconsistent colouring.

4

Put on your rubber gloves. Steep the fabric in the dye, all the way up to the masking tape. Try to submerge the fabric evenly so the dye line is straight. Agitate the fabric with a stick as often as possible and try to eliminate folds. Leave the pillowcase in the dye for around 10 minutes.

5

After 10 minutes, lift the fabric up by about one-third, then leave for another 10 minutes.

6

After the second 10 minutes, lift the fabric up by another third, leaving the last third of the fabric in the dye. This will be the darkest part of the pillowcase. The longer you leave it in, the darker it will be.

7

Remove the pillowcase and wash the dyed end thoroughly (using washing powder) until the water runs clear. This may take a while, but it's really important to get all the excess dye out to prevent the pillowcase staining things when it's wet.

Remove the plastic bag from the plain end of the pillowcase, dry the pillowcase and enjoy!

1

T-SHIRT

Wash and dry the t-shirt. Lay out the newspaper and place the t-shirt flat on top. Place the thick cardboard inside the t-shirt to prevent bleach soaking through to the other side.

2

If you have a test piece of dark fabric, experiment by using different objects to apply the bleach and see how the marks work with the fabric. When you are ready, start applying bleach to your t-shirt.

3

The bleach should begin to work in a few minutes. Fabrics react to bleach in different ways – thinner fabrics react faster than thicker ones, but may cause the bleach to bleed more.

When you are finished, leave the t-shirt to dry – it won't take long.

4

Turn the t-shirt over and repeat the bleach marks on the back. You don't want to leave the bleach on the fabric for too long as it can corrode it, so try to finish in under 20 minutes. Thoroughly wash the fabric, by hand or in the washing machine, then dry.

Tip

Not all dark fabrics will bleach the same colour – try a tiny test patch on your t-shirt first to see what colour it will bleach out.

Please consider wearing gloves while working with bleach!

GIFT WRAP SET

{ DIFFICULTY: medium }

I just love wrapping presents, so much so that when I'm shopping and someone offers to gift wrap for me, I usually say no. Even at Christmas time! Since I live in a relatively disorganised household, however, I often find I am without wrapping paper, so I have come up with some inventive ways to make my own.

I have used plain brown packing paper as the base here, because it's easy to find (try your newsagent) and something I always have on hand.

YOU WILL NEED

- templates (page 226)
- pink/teal/beige/green/coral card (thin enough to fold)
- scissors
- pink gouache paint
- paintbrush
- double-sided tape or glue
- washi tape
- brown packing paper
- potatoes
- stanley knife
- coral/pink/green acrylic paints
- paintbrush or sponge

LET'S GET STARTED

1

For the envelope use the templates on page 226 and trace the envelope pieces onto different-coloured card.

2

Use scissors to cut out both of the copied templates.

3

Paint some diagonal stripes in pink gouache onto one side of the outer envelope piece. Alternatively create your own pattern or design.

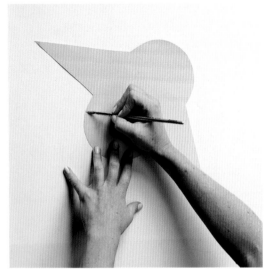

4

Using some double-sided tape or glue, stick the inner envelope piece to the side of the outer envelope piece without stripes. Use the picture as a guide to help you.

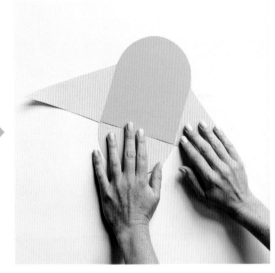

5

Score the envelope as indicated on the template, then fold into shape so that the stripes are on the outside. Fasten the bottom of the envelope with double-sided tape or glue.

6

For the rosette, trace and cut all the parts of the card templates onto different-coloured card.

7

When you are done, your cut-outs should look like this.

8

Use washi tape or different-coloured card to make a stripe on the ribbon parts of the rosette. Stick all the pieces together, attaching the ribbon parts to the back of the rosette. I have added a pale-blue polka dot to the circle in the centre of the rosette.

1

For the wrapping paper, cut your potatoes in half, then use a stanley knife to cut out shapes on the flat side of each, making sure the shapes are quite raised. I have made three stamps – a triangle, a cross and a semi-circle.

Apply paint to your stamps using a paintbrush or sponge. It's a good idea to give your stamps a few test prints before going ahead with your final wrapping paper.

2

Roll out a length of paper and start stamping!

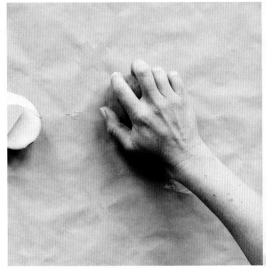

3

Leave the first colour to dry before applying the next colour. This can take time, but it's the best way to avoid smudging your stamps.

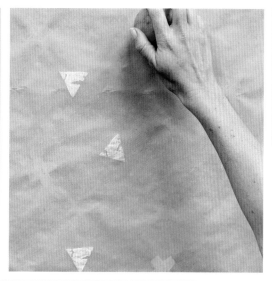

4

When all the colours have been applied, leave the paper to dry for a final time. If your paper is buckling as it absorbs the paint, place some heavy books on it overnight to help flatten it out.

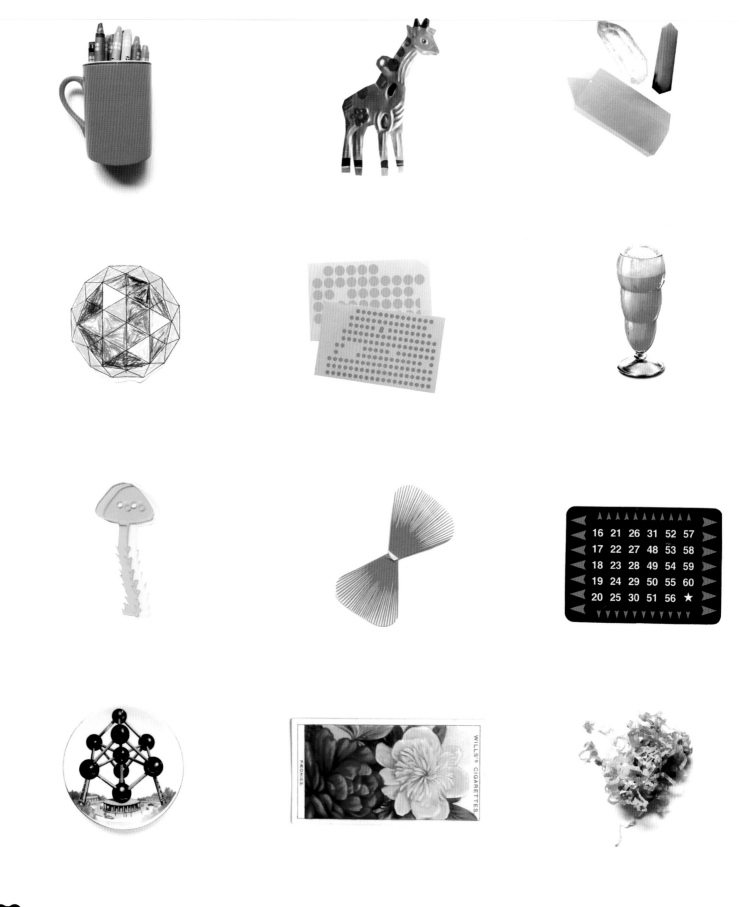

POM POM MANIA

{ DIFFICULTY: easy }

Can you think of anything that doesn't look better when a pom pom is added? I can't. I put them on cushions, turn them into toys for cats and even wear them as a headpiece! They are ridiculously easy and rewarding to make, too. If you are planning to make pom poms en masse (and why wouldn't you?), you may want to invest in pom pom makers. They are relatively cheap and easy to use, and will double your efficiency.

I find it's easiest to cut the wool into manageable lengths, say 1–2 metres (40–80 in), or you'll get into quite a tangle. When each length of wool ends, just leave it sticking out and start winding the next piece around. The more wool you wrap, the fuller your pom pom will be (I like mine really full). Using a different-coloured wool every now and then gives a great effect too.

You can enlarge or shrink the template to make different-sized pom poms.

YOU WILL NEED

- pom pom template (page 227) copied onto thick cardboard
- sharp scissors
- approximately 20 metres (65 ft 7 in) wool
- masking tape

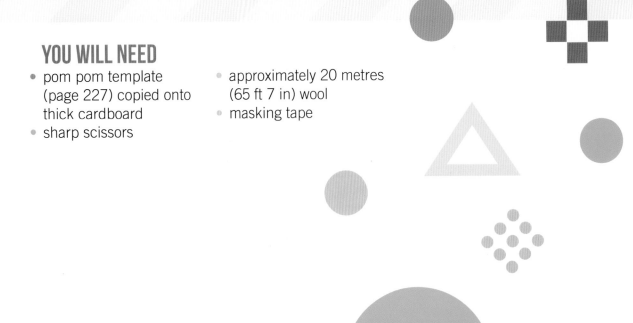

1

Cut out the two template shapes and place one on top of the other. Cut the wool into manageable lengths. Secure the end of a piece of wool to the cardboard with masking tape and begin threading it around and through the centre. Continue until the card is quite full.

2

When your 'donut' is full it's time to cut it. Cut in between the two pieces of card, which can be slightly tricky. You really do need to use sharp scissors for this, as it may take a few snips to get through the wool. Just cut a few layers at a time.

3

When all the wool is cut, run another length of wool between the two cardboard templates and tie it firmly, leaving one end long.

4

Remove the cardboard templates. The easiest way to do this is to cut them.

5

Trim any uneven strands of wool.

6

Some ideas for pom poms:
- attach to twigs and put in a vase.
- use hot glue or wool to attach to a headband for a cute headpiece.
- tie onto cord to create a garland.
- sew onto the corners of a blanket.

WOODEN BLOCK FAMILY

{ DIFFICULTY: medium }

Although most of my work is two-dimensional, I also love to work in 3-D.
I have often painted wooden objects for parts of my exhibitions and
they always end up being my favourite bits. The wooden shapes in my
exhibitions are custom-made, but it's just as easy to create something
similar using regular wooden blocks. They can be recycled or offcut pieces
(try your local hardware store) or you could buy a set of children's wooden
blocks (preferably natural wood, not painted). Play around with the
expressions you give them to make different personalities, as this will make
the interactions between them lots of fun.

For the wood varnish, I use a water-based polyurethane varnish in a satin
finish, available from craft stores.

YOU WILL NEED

- wooden blocks
- sandpaper, if required
- pencil
- acrylic paint
- paintbrushes
- eraser
- wood varnish

LET'S GET STARTED

1

Smooth off the blocks using sandpaper if necessary. You can also use sandpaper to remove varnish. The blocks I used had varnish on them, but as they were quite old I was able to paint over it. I liked their worn look and didn't want to lose this.

2

Pencil out your ideas – draw the rough shapes of your blocks and have a play with different patterns and faces within the shapes. Think about colours and have a play around with the paints you have chosen.

3

Draw your designs on the blocks lightly in pencil. Don't press heavily as you may leave a permanent impression on the wood.

4

Start painting. It can take a few goes to get used to painting the wood, so I usually keep a practice block to test colours and different paintbrushes on. This makes starting the final pieces less intimidating!

5

When you have finished painting, set the blocks aside to dry, then erase any visible pencil lines. Pencil can show through some light-coloured paints, but I like this – it adds to the hand-painted effect. You can cover it up with extra coats of paint, if you prefer.

6

If your blocks are going to be used by children, give them a few coats of varnish. This will also give your pieces a polished appearance. Once finished, go forth and build your wooden block empire!

VINTAGE POSTCARD ART

{ DIFFICULTY: medium }

Collage is one of my favourite mediums, simply because it's so easy. I use it all the time while compiling things in my sketchbook, and in final pieces, too. I even make virtual collages on my computer, piecing together my own drawings, shapes and images. It's endless fun!

Here are some ideas for how to put together your own collages. I've used two contrasting elements: soft-feeling vintage photos and bright clean shapes and lines.

I purposely chose photos with different subjects: a landscape, a person and a ship. I also chose three that are in the portrait position and have a similar feel (ie, around the same era). But you can do whatever you like!

When you are buying paints, papers and embroidery thread, choose similar colours – this will make the collages come together as a set or series.

YOU WILL NEED

- 3 vintage photos or postcards
- coloured paper
- plain coloured sticker shapes
- scissors
- glue
- paint
- paintbrush
- embroidery thread
- needle
- frame (optional)

LET'S GET STARTED

1

Look at your pictures and sketch up ideas for each. Consider adding geometric shapes, a centred pattern, painted elements, or embroidered lines or stars. You could also play around with figurative touches such as rosy cheeks on people, a paper hat or bow tie on an animal, or a rainbow.

2

Try some of the ideas by placing them on the pictures first, experimenting with different locations. Remember, there is no right or wrong with this project. As long as you take your time and trust your creative instincts you will end up with something beautiful.

3

When you have made your decision for each photo, proceed with the final pieces – stick down paper and complete embroidering.

4

Frame your cards, if you like, then hang them and bask in the glory of your art-making! If they buckle slightly after applying glue, place them under heavy books overnight. Or leave them as they are – I think a slight buckling can add movement and look beautiful.

INSPIRATION WALL

{ DIFFICULTY: easy }

It's no secret, I'm a chronic hoarder. But I'm a hoarder with rhyme and reason. I use the things I hoard – I look at them and decorate with them. Plus, I keep them organised, which makes them look like collections rather than a random mess.

Creating inspiration walls is one way I put my hoarded objects to good use. They look pretty, too. I create them all the time in my studio, often by accident but sometimes intentionally as well, to help with particular projects I'm working on.

When it comes to choosing the objects you put on your wall, a good place to start is a selection of postcards, flyers, ribbons, coloured paper, artwork, stickers – anything that catches your eye and can be easily stuck to a wall. Think outside the square, too. Three-dimensional objects can also work well – try kids' toys, clothing, pom poms, jewellery and so on.

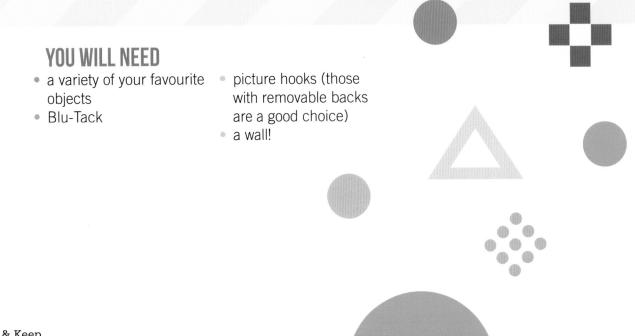

YOU WILL NEED

- a variety of your favourite objects
- Blu-Tack
- picture hooks (those with removable backs are a good choice)
- a wall!

LET'S GET STARTED

1

Gather your collection of 'inspirational' objects. You might like to start with a theme, which could be as simple as a few colours (say, red, blue and yellow) or something more specific like 'vintage kids' stuff'. Themes sometimes occur organically as you bring your objects together.

necktie

2

Choose one of your favourite things as the starting point and stick it on the wall.

3

Select some more objects to go around your first object. Consider things such as the colours or shape of your first object, and see if you can match or complement that with the next few objects you place around it.

4

Continue to add bits and pieces, building out from the first piece.

5

When you think there are enough objects on the wall and you are happy with how it's looking, leave it for a minute and go and have a cup of tea.

6

Once you are happy (for a final time!), sit back and enjoy.

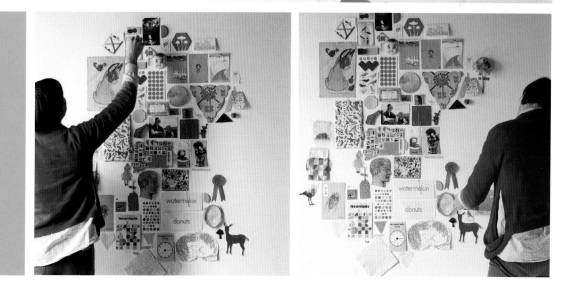

BUNNY EMBROIDERY

{ DIFFICULTY: medium }

I am a big fan of embroidery. I have a box in my collections dedicated just to embroidered pieces I've found in op-shops and the like. To be honest, my own embroidery skills are pretty amateur and up until now I've only really dabbled in it, with a few framed pieces and spruced-up t-shirts. But even my amateur stitching is something I find very rewarding and therapeutic (especially when combined with some good TV and red wine!). It's like drawing in slow motion.

I have used the finished bunny design as a framed piece on a wall, but it would also look nice on a tea towel or even on the chest pocket of your favourite shirt.

Although plain fabric is the base for this project, the design could work well on a simple pattern, too. The tracing technique I have used will only work on lighter coloured fabrics.

YOU WILL NEED

- traced or photocopied bunny template (page 227)
- pencil
- light fabric for the base
- embroidery hoop (14.5 cm/6 in or so, preferably wooden)
- embroidery thread
- scissors
- picture hook

LET'S GET STARTED

1

Trace the design onto the fabric. I did this with a pencil by placing the photocopied design behind the fabric and then the fabric over the top. This technique will only work with light-coloured fabrics.

2

Place the fabric in the embroidery hoop and fasten it. Stretch the fabric as taut as possible. Start with the centre rabbit motif. I used full embroidery thread and a small backstitch for the outline (see stitch guide on page 227).

3

When the outline is done, proceed with the rest of the embroidery. Do all the outlines first, then the fill-ins. You can fill in more parts than I did – in fact, do whatever you like! For areas requiring fill-ins, I used a (pretty messy) satin stitch.

4

When it's finished, you can just about pop it on the wall straight away – the hoop even provides an instant frame! I use a few rough stitches to tuck the overhanging fabric behind it, but you can also trim it down and use a bit of tape to tuck it out of the way.

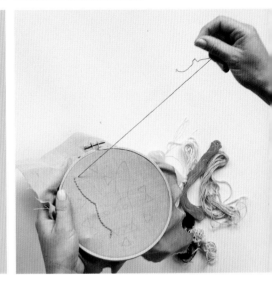

Tip

Try experimenting
with different
stitches for
different parts of
the embroidery.
My colour
selection is
only a guide;
choose your own
to match your
house!

3D PAPER SHAPES

{ DIFFICULTY: medium }

There are some amazing paper artists around today, and the things they make are pretty incredible. Because I love working with paper, I've tried my hand with a bit of three-dimensional folding. Paper folding can be quite tricky, but these simple shapes are a good project for beginners.

As for what to do with them when you are finished, how about filling them with cute little gifts, adding them to an inspiration wall, or using them as parts of a mobile. Or they could just look pretty on your coffee table.

YOU WILL NEED

- scissors
- traced or photocopied shape templates (page 230)
- coloured card
- stanley knife
- ruler
- patterned paper (optional)
- watercolour paint/inks
- paintbrushes
- glue or double-sided tape

LET'S GET STARTED

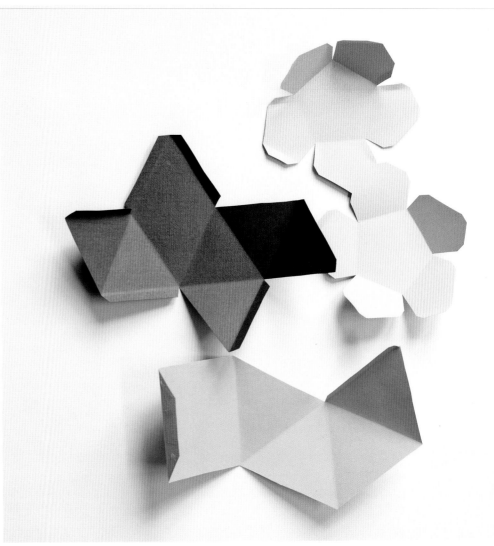

1

Cut out the shape templates on coloured card and, using a stanley knife and ruler, score and fold them as indicated on the templates. Make sure you fold all the folds in the same direction.

2

I like to add coloured panels to each shape. If your shapes are made using plain paper, try patterned panels or paper painted with watercolours or inks. Trace one shape section from the template, cut out and stick onto the side that will be facing out.

3

Before sticking the template together, fold it into the final shape so you can understand how it fits.

Add double-sided tape or glue to all the tab sections of the template and fold back together. This can be tricky and takes a bit of patience. If you are using the shape as a gift box, leave one panel unstuck and mark this panel with pencil before folding.

5

If using as a gift box, make sure the section which will open has a strong crease so it will stay in place. Fill with a tiny present before fastening.

HOME

My obsession with personalising my space started young. At around 14, I decided I wanted my bedroom to have a minimalist warehouse look, so I tore up the floral carpet to reveal the bare unpolished floorboards and convinced my mum all I needed in my room was a clothes rack and a double bed with a perfectly placed mosquito net above. It wasn't long before I discovered minimalism was not my thing. I loved 'stuff' too much. Since then, I haven't looked back.

I am still obsessive about personalising my space, and 'stuff'. The difference now is I get to spread out into a whole house, not just my bedroom! This can be a dangerous situation and one which I am only now getting the hang of. I'm slowly learning the art of editing, or 'unstuffing'!

Most of my 'stuff' is not particularly expensive. Yes, I have invested in some nice chairs and artwork, but a lot of it also comes from flea markets, op-shops, and the odd bit of hard rubbish, too. I think that is how you can create the best personality in a home – not worrying about where things come from, just worrying about whether you love them or not.

More and more, I'm appreciating the non-perfect side of house decorating. I can easily spend hours rearranging my 'stuff' – adding, subtracting, moving things around – until it looks just about perfect. Then I leave it for a few days, let my kids do their own rearranging, let the family mess accrue around it, and let it get lived in. And that's when I like these arrangements most.

FAVOURITE SHOPS

These days, to spend even a few hours simply shopping is a real luxury for me. When I get to do it, I lap it up. Even if I'm just looking around, my favourite stores can give me ideas. I love how the curation of products and shop displays inspire me to make things at home.

I like seeking things out myself, but it's also nice when someone else has done the hard work for you. I'm a sucker for hand-crafted products. Even if they cost a little more, I'd much prefer to save up my pennies than buy something mass-produced.

I love kids' art! Its spontaneity and untamed-ness has a quality that is hard to find elsewhere. I enjoy making things with my kids, and find it really satisfying, too – for all of us. My son Ari and I often get down to some craft on our days hanging out. He is always so proud of what he makes – it's awesome! This little project was something of a collaboration between us. I have a small (and growing) collection of vintage pennants. Ari was quite interested in them for a while, so we decided to make one for his room.

DO NOT TOUCH THE CATERPILLERS an TREE

Tyke

Ari painted some paper with inks (his current preferred medium) which was to be the background of the flag.

He also chose the coloured paper for his name, and then I did the cutting and sticking and everything else.

PENNANT

We were both impressed with how it turned out. After a while, my other son Tyke wanted one above his bed!

LOUNGE

When I go to an op-shop, the first place I visit is the fabrics section (followed closely by bric-a-brac). I can't resist a cheap fabric in a pretty colour, and have gathered a good collection. I'm happy for the fabrics just to sit on my shelves (I can easily spend an hour or two re-arranging the colour orders), but every now and again I run out of shelf space, so I use some of the fabrics to make simple diagonal cushions. I have sold these cushions at markets, but this time they were for my house. I had bought a new rug with lots of nice pink and taupe tones, and I wanted some cushions to roughly match. I started by cutting out some small paper triangles in similar colours to the rug – it's an easy way to work out colour combinations before you cut the pattern pieces. Then I cut out a few of the triangle pattern pieces from the fabric and played around with them, also looking at wool colours (for later pom pom additions), until the right combinations popped out at me.

I'll let you in on a secret – I'm really bad at sewing!

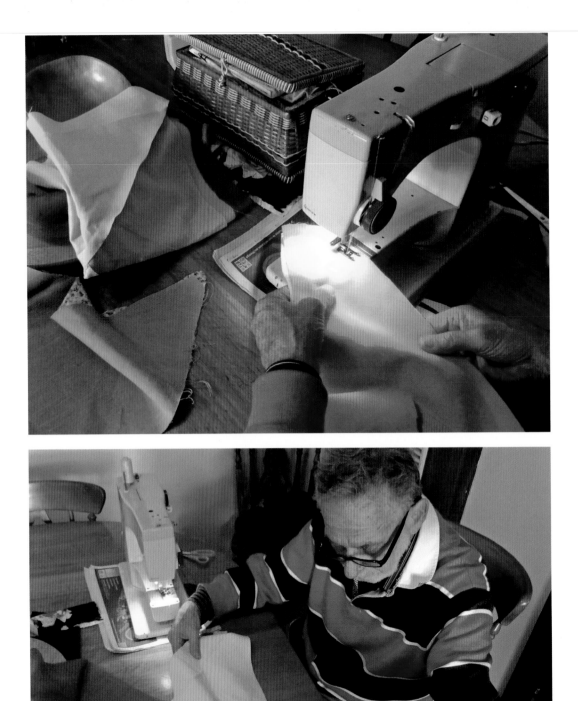

Lucky for me my stepdad Erwin used to be a tailor, so I took the cut pattern pieces to him and he whipped up the cushions for me in under 10 minutes.

CUSHIONS

With the right-coloured pom pom as the final touch, the cushions were ready for the lounge room.

GRAPHIC

I know my husband Raph's aesthetic pretty well by now, so when he asked me late one night to develop a label for his new chilli sauce (and some other things he had been making), I happily rose to the challenge. A collection of objects from Raph's desk is an easy giveaway of what he likes: font-based graphics with an American vintage feel, especially ones that have been adapted to include a sense of humour. Throw in an ethnic twist, a few hand-drawn elements and that pretty much covers Raph's style.

Raph wanted the label to be in a similar style to his food trucks Beatbox Kitchen and the Taco Truck (which I also designed), as he wanted the chilli sauce to be served in both trucks.

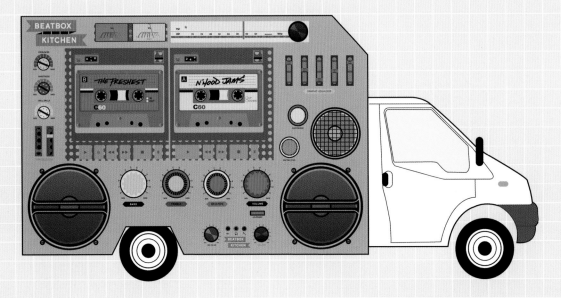

I started by looking at our collection of signage photos and graphics that we've collected over the years. Here are a few of Raph's which pointed me in the right direction for his label.

Using this collection as well as images of vintage type I had collected from the internet, I created Raph's font. He didn't want it to be cursive, but quite plain and with its own personality. I think adding the serifs to the font helped achieve this.

LABEL

The surrounding black shape is a mix of graphics taken from the Taco Truck and Beatbox Kitchen. We finished it in under two hours and Raph really loved it. The advantages of having an in-house graphic designer, hey?

SAKURA CRAY-PAS ふとまき16色

SAKURA

HOME
PROJECTS

Now it's
time to add some
of yourself to your own house!
The following projects should give you
some good starting points. Most of them are
inexpensive ways to create lovely (and sometimes
useful) things for your house. Of course, you can just use
my instructions as a guide – feel free to interpret them as
personally as you wish. The more personal you make them, the
more successful you will be in adding a bit of you to your home.

PAPER GARLAND

{ DIFFICULTY: easy }

Everybody loves a garland! Well, I do, anyway. And not just for a party decoration – they are a cheap, easy and pretty way to add an element of fun to a room.

The variations for garlands are endless, but this project will get you started. It is my 'geometric shape' garland. As well as using coloured paper, I've painted some paper with inks and watercolours to add a bit more interest. I also painted some paper with simple patterns using gouache paint, and used fluorescent cotton to string it all together.

YOU WILL NEED

- watercolour paper
- watercolour paints
- drawing inks
- acrylic or gouache paint
- paintbrushes
- traced or photocopied shape templates (page 230)
- coloured card
- pencil
- scissors
- approximately 4 metres (13 ft) cotton
- glue

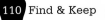

LET'S GET STARTED

1

Paint some sheets of watercolour paper. I like to use watercolour paint at one end and then a different colour of ink at the other. Apply the watercolour first. I change the consistency of the paint by adding more or less water – this gives a nice texture.

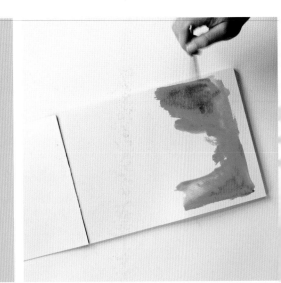

2

Add the ink (or second watercolour) to the other end of the paper and work down with your brush towards the middle. Work quickly so the first colour doesn't dry before you touch it with the second colour.

3

Add some patterns to your sheets of plain card with a contrasting colour of paint. Try polka dots, triangles, stripes, squares – anything simple and bold will work well.

4

Trace the shape templates onto the paper. For this project, I made templates out of thicker card first as they were going to be getting a lot of use.

5

Mix and match the shapes and colours you cut out. I cut an even amount of each shape and colour, but you can choose different combinations, if you wish.

6

Sort your shapes according to colour. This makes it easier when you are attaching them to the cotton, especially if you want a certain order. I attached my shapes randomly, but wanted to make sure there was a good mix of shape and colour.

7

Attach cotton to your shapes with glue. If you don't have enough space to spread out the garland as it dries, just glue a few shapes at a time. When they have dried completely, stack them up and continue gluing until the garland is complete.

TINY TOWN

{ DIFFICULTY: easy }

This is obviously a project that would be fun to make with kids, if you happen to have some around. But don't let that stop you if not – big kids are allowed to have fun, too!

Tiny towns look awesome in between pot plants or on a bookshelf. And the best part of a tiny town is that you're the boss. You can make it summer at any time of the year. Create controversial new high-rise developments, or a whole street filled with lolly shops. That kind of thing. Your tiny town is your oyster. Hours of fun at any age.

YOU WILL NEED

- pencil
- traced or photocopied tiny town templates (pages 227–8)
- thick card (we used pasteboard)
- cutting mat (optional, but handy)
- scalpel or stanley knife
- acrylic paint
- sticky tape

LET'S GET STARTED

1

Use a pencil to trace your templates onto the thick card.

2

Place the card on a cutting mat if you have one, and cut out the shapes using a scalpel or stanley knife. If you would like super-straight edges, you could use a ruler when cutting. Try drawing your own buildings, too. You are the boss, remember – it's all about you.

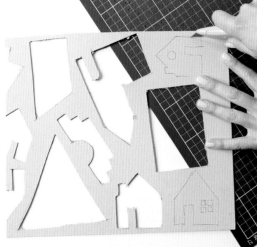

3

When the outside shapes are cut out, start to cut out the smaller details (such as windows) of the separate shapes.

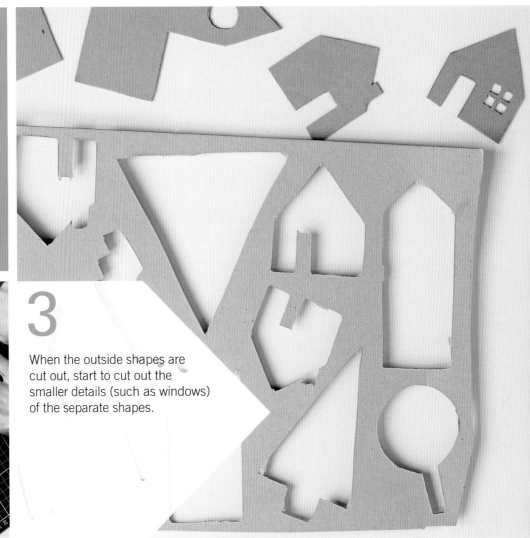

4

Paint your town pieces. When painting my pieces, I kept it very simple with block colours. It could be cute to add more details, such as shop signs, roof tiles, ivy growing up buildings and so on.

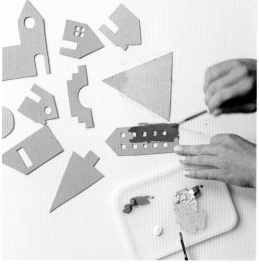

5

When the paint has dried, attach the triangle stands to the back of the pieces with tape. Add one piece of tape to each side of the stands.

6

When you have attached the tape to both sides of the stands, they should hold in place and your building should stand up.

BUNNY VS ROBOT MASKS

{ DIFFICULTY: easy }

Masks are a little bit scary, but a whole lot awesome. I've had a fascination with them for a while, and a few years ago I made a series of prints based around good and evil girls, all wearing masks.

They are fun to wear for both young and old, but I also like sticking them on the wall as a decoration. I have four masks on my living room wall – it freaked my kids out for a while, but they learned to live with it. You could do the same with these ones if you like.

For the card, I used the following colours: gold glitter, pale aqua blue, purple, olive, yellow and mid-blue.

YOU WILL NEED

- traced or photocopied templates (pages 232–3)
- pencil
- coloured and metallic card
- scissors
- paper confetti (optional)
- glue
- small pom pom (for bunny nose)
- elastic

LET'S GET STARTED

1

Trace all the mask component templates onto the coloured cards.

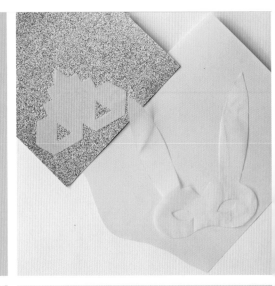

2

Cut out all the mask components. Double check you have all the pieces. If you are using confetti you will not need to cut out the circle pieces.

3

As there are quite a few pieces, it's easy to get them confused. If you are making both masks at the same time, sort the components into separate piles: one for the bunny and one for the robot.

4

Glue the decorations onto the mask base – use the final picture (opposite) as a guide. For the rabbit, glue the confetti pieces around the eyes and the biggest V-shape at the top of the face first, as these bits have other parts that sit on top.

5

If you are using glitter card for the robot, it can take a fair bit of glue to stick other paper on top.

6

Attach elastic by piercing a small hole in each side and tying it through.

Tip
If your rabbit's ears are flopping down, you can prop them up by taping skewers or chopsticks to the back.

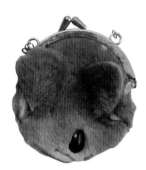

  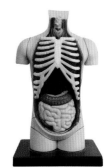

DREAM CATCHER

{ DIFFICULTY: medium }

My son Ari is obsessed with dream catchers. He made one out of pipe cleaners and feathers at kindy one day. It was excellent, and he truly believed it took his bad dreams away. Quite handy, really! Although I do encourage a bit of new-age thinking with my kids, I cannot guarantee this dream catcher will actually catch bad dreams. I can guarantee it will look pretty, though.

You can attach different objects to the bottom of the dream catcher – try pom poms, charms or anything else that is light and attractive.

For the hoop, I used an embroidery hoop from my local craft store.

YOU WILL NEED
- cotton doily that roughly fits inside the hoop
- ink for dyeing (optional)
- double-sided tape
- metal hoop
- embroidery thread in different colours
- feathers
- wooden beads

LET'S GET STARTED

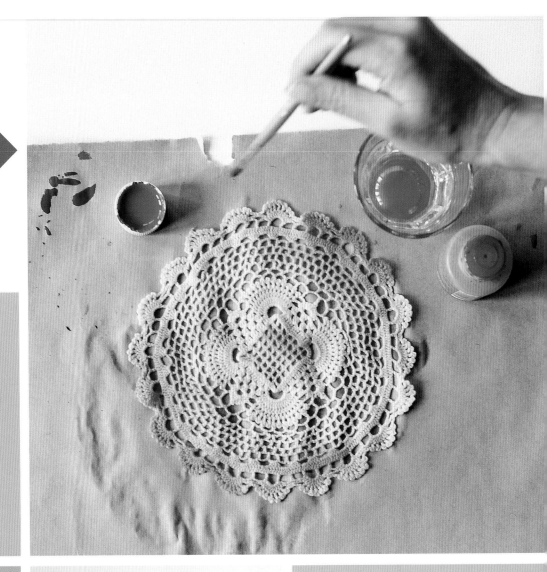

1

If you wish to dye your doily, do this first. I painted mine with drawing ink and went for a mottled tie-dye look.
A plain doily still looks pretty, and we have used one in the following steps.

2

Wrap some double-sided tape around the hoop. Just do a little bit at a time. Tightly wrap embroidery thread around the hoop to cover it (the tape will keep it in place) – I have used blocks of different-coloured thread.

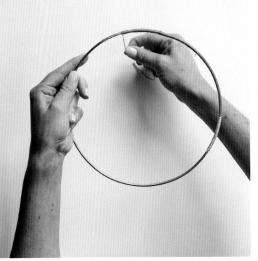

3

Wind some embroidery thread around the ends of the feathers, using double-sided tape and a knot to secure it. I used three lengths of embroidery thread in different colours for each feather. Leave some extra length for plaiting.

4

Plait the embroidery thread on the feathers. I used a piece of masking tape to stabilise the feather while I did the plaiting.

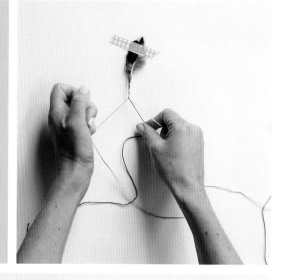

5

Add the beads to the plaited thread on the feathers. Tie a knot to secure the beads.

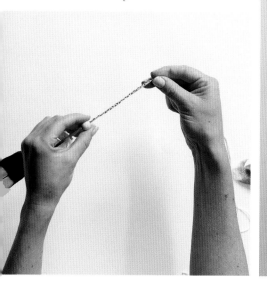

6

Tie the feathers to the hoop.

7

Tie the doily to the hoop. I tied it in eight evenly spaced places to keep it secure.

8

Attach a loop of embroidery thread to the top of the dream catcher so you can hang it up.

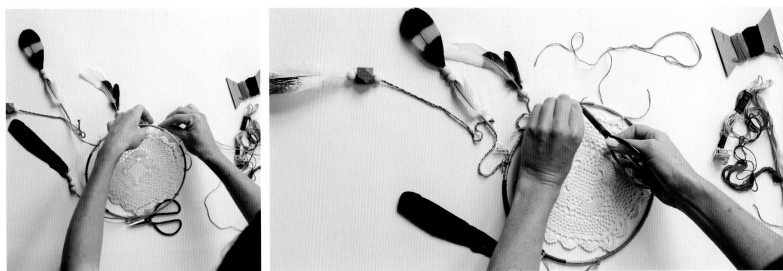

CAKE STENCIL

{ DIFFICULTY: easy }

Have you ever visited a cake decorating shop? If not, I strongly suggest you do so, ASAP! Even if you don't like baking, these places will inspire you to create something amazing.

A visit to my local cake decorating shop inspired this project. I was particularly taken aback by the huge range of edible glitter available, and needed to find something to do with it. The glitter range was even called 'disco', which made me like it even more. Plus, it's super easy to use.

This project is all about the glitter, not the baking, so feel free to use it on a bought cake. Either way, it's sure to add a bit of disco to your afternoon tea. And that is a very good thing!

YOU WILL NEED

- traced or photocopied template (page 229) or your own design
- sheet of acetate
- stanley knife
- cutting board
- iced cake (we used a buttercream frosting)
- edible glitter in 3 colours

LET'S GET STARTED

1

Place the template under the acetate and cut out the design.

2

Position the stencil gently over the cake. Warm icing is more likely to stick to the acetate, so keep your cake in the fridge until you are ready to stencil.

3

Using the template or image on the opposite page as a guide, sprinkle over your first colour with your fingertips – the glitter will be very fine.

4

Sprinkle over your second colour. Be careful not to let the acetate stencil slip from the cake.

5

Sprinkle over your third colour, then carefully remove the stencil.

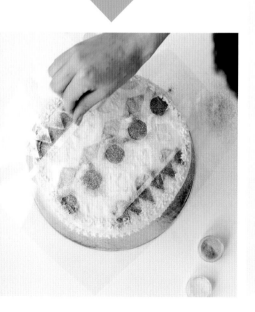

GIANT CONFETTI WALL

{ DIFFICULTY: easy }

Confetti has become a bit of a rarity these days. The proper old-school tissue paper kind, anyway. Whenever I find a newsagent that carries it, I buy up big, and subsequently have a small cupboard full of confetti boxes. My son Ari discovered these boxes one day and had a fantastic time spreading confetti all over my studio, until I discovered him and broke up the party (and it did look like a party – a really big one at that!).

In the following weeks, while I continued to find confetti in every nook and cranny of my studio, I came up with this idea. Here's how you can make your room look like a party – a much cleaner version than Ari's, but just as much fun.

YOU WILL NEED

- lots of different coloured paper and card (scraps will do fine)
- traced or photocopied circle template (page 227)
- scissors
- Blu-Tack
- a wall!

LET'S GET STARTED

1

Gather your paper together. Scraps of paper of different colours and textures will work very well.

2

Using the template as a guide, cut out as many circles as possible from your coloured card.

3

Once you have cut out all the circles, arrange them roughly by colour. This will help you get organised and it looks nice, too.

4

Using Blu-Tack on the back of the circles, start sticking them onto the wall. Start with one circle and try to make the other circles look like they are floating away from that point in different directions.

5

Continue until all your circles are on the wall. On corners or where the wall meets the floor, use half-circles with the flat edge flush against the straight line. These details create an overall better effect for your confetti wall.

GIRL & BEAR MOBILE

{ DIFFICULTY: hard }

I have made quite a few mobiles in my time – for exhibitions, to sell on my website, or to have at home. I think they are great story-telling vessels.

This one tells the forlorn tale of a bear who is in love with a girl. He pursues her relentlessly (as only a bear knows how). Unfortunately for him, the girl does not return his love. Here, she is telling him off and about to threaten him with an arrow (a pursuing bear can be a little aggressive!), while the poor old bear reaches out his arms in hope.

You can recreate this tale of unrequited love or make up your own version of the story in this mobile.

YOU WILL NEED

- watercolour paper
- paintbrushes
- pink and aqua drawing inks
- traced or photocopied templates (page 233)
- scissors
- card in different colours (pale pink, olive, yellow)
- paint (gouache or acrylic)
- double-sided tape or glue
- small split pins
- embroidery thread
- a thin piece of dowel

LET'S GET STARTED

1

Make some sheets of ink-washed paper in pink and aqua (look at the paper garland project on page 112 for more instructions). When they are dry, gather all the paper together. Use the pink for the girl's hair and one of the bear's arms, and the aqua for the girl's arms and the bear's face.

2

Using the copied templates, cut out all your pieces from the paper and coloured card. Many of the pieces need doubles – for these pieces, cut on the fold as shown.

3

Organise all the pieces to make sure you are not missing any parts.

4

Paint details onto the bodies, such as small dots on the girl's jumpsuit and fur on the bear.

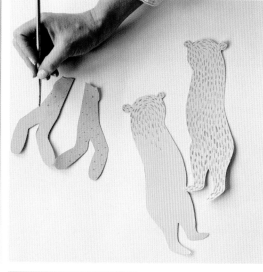

5

For each side of the bear's body, first glue down the face and then affix the constructed arms with a split pin.

6

Attach embroidery thread to the reverse side of the bear's body and then stick the two body parts together, sandwiching the thread in between. Make sure you don't add glue around the pin area, as the pins need to be able to move around.

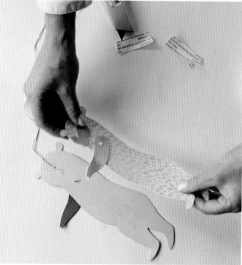

7

Construct the girl's arms – use glue to attach her hands to each arm so they are sandwiched between the two arm pieces.

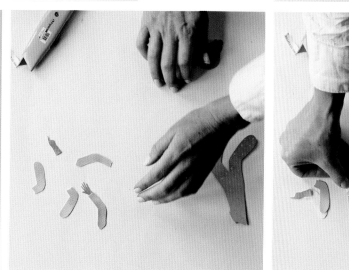

8

Construct the girl's body –
sandwich her feet and head pieces
in between the jumpsuit, then stick
the jumpsuit pieces together to hold
everything in place.

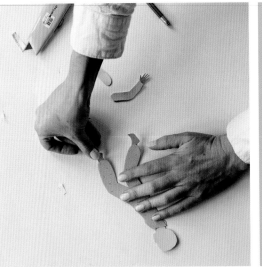

9

Place embroidery thread on one of
the inside-facing pieces of the hair,
then attach the hair pieces to either
side of the face with the embroidery
thread sandwiched in between.

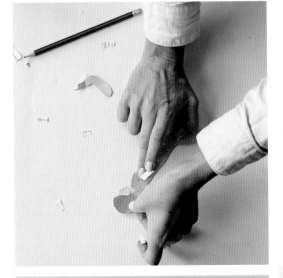

10

Add the shapes to the thread
– again, so they sandwich the
thread in between them.

11

Tie the thread with the attached
pieces to the dowel. It can take a bit
of tweaking to balance the mobile.
Tying it initially allows you to move
the parts around; when you have the
mobile balanced, glue it all in place.

CROSS-STITCHED COAT HOOK

{ DIFFICULTY: easy }

I like making pretty things, especially pretty things with a function. I cannot lay claim to inventing this project – the inspiration came from my vast collection of 70s craft books. But I have put my own spin on it.

The materials in this project are easy to find, but it does require some sawing. I used my (very handy) dad, who's a builder, but you might be able to convince someone at your local hardware store to do it. If you want to do the sawing yourself, go for it. Pegboard is easy to cut, but please be careful! Severed fingers and craft are not a good match.

Our piece of pegboard was 120 x 90 cm (47 x 35 in) and we cut it into thirds. The beads I used were 18 mm (¾ in), with 6 mm (¼ in) holes.

YOU WILL NEED

- measuring tape
- piece of pegboard
- pencil
- saw (if cutting the pegboard yourself)
- different-coloured wool
- masking tape
- stitch guide (page 227)
- 4 pegboard hooks
- 4 wooden beads (to fit on the hooks)

LET'S GET STARTED

1

Measure out your desired length of pegboard and mark with pencil.

2

Carefully saw your pegboard along the marked line (thanks Dad!).

3

Place your pegboard on something that will make it easy to thread into (we used a stool). Cut approximately 2 metres (6 ft 7 in) of wool.

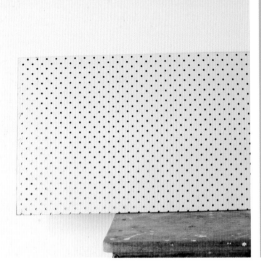

4

Attach tape to the ends of the wool to make it easier to thread through the holes (you could also use a darning needle). Tie a knot at the other end of the wool to prevent it pulling through.

5

Thread the wool through the pegboard and start to cross-stitch. I used a different colour for each letter. You can choose your own word instead of 'hello' – just make sure you map out how many letters will fit across your board before you start!

6

Once complete, attach the hooks to the bottom row of holes, then add beads to the hook ends. The beads I used stuck quite easily by just pushing them down, but you could secure them with glue or Blu-Tack in the bead hole if you like.

PRETTY PICTURES

{ DIFFICULTY: easy }

One day, I was rushing to send a belated birthday package to my sister Emily, who lives across the ocean. I had her presents all wrapped and ready to go, then at the last moment I decided she needed something more personal. I found some photos that Tyke and Ari had taken of themselves with a polaroid camera and put them in a frame. But it was boring! It needed a quick hit with the cute stick.

After a scurry around my studio, I added just a few bits – suddenly, it looked so much nicer! Even I was surprised by how a few pieces of scrap paper could make something look so much better. Emily thought so, too – she emailed me later saying it was her favourite present in the package (and that's the last time I buy her a limited-edition Miu Miu handbag!).

YOU WILL NEED

- scissors
- coloured card
- picture frame
- coloured circle stickers
- box of confetti, or other cut-out geometric shapes
- photo
- glue

LET'S GET STARTED

1

Cut your coloured card down to size so it fits your chosen picture frame.

2

Separate the shapes and play around with the way they will sit on the coloured card base.

3

Put the photos in position. I chose to have the circles look like they are floating down from the top left corner of the frame.

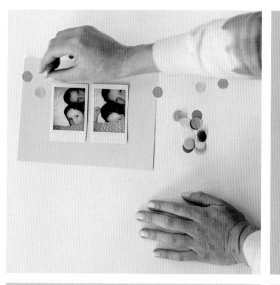

4

Try adding some shapes on top of the photo as well as underneath to give more interest and depth.

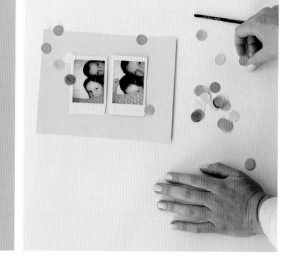

5

When you are happy with your arrangement, remove the photos and stick down your shapes.

6

Stick down your photos and add any shapes you would like to place on top. Once dry, put your completed piece in the frame.

FAUX LEADLIGHT

{ DIFFICULTY: medium }

The windows in the houses where I grew up were quite leadlight-heavy. My stepfather even had a little leadlight studio in his garage. So it is a craft I've been familiar with for a long time. Like many things you grow up with, I was pretty much revolted by it – until recently. But now that we are planning our own renovation, we are making space for our own leadlight windows... Beci-style, though!

I used a mix of coloured adhesive vinyl and coloured tracing paper in this project. The vinyl can be tricky to find – I ended up buying mine through a sign writer, and it wasn't cheap. But coloured tracing paper and acetate stuck down with double-sided tape will create a similar effect.

I have opted for random shapes and colours together, which is a tricky combination. If you prefer the same shapes and colours in each star, it will be easier to assemble.

YOU WILL NEED

- transparent coloured adhesive vinyl and/or coloured tracing paper and colour acetate
- traced or photocopied template (page 231)
- stanley knife/scalpel
- ruler
- cutting mat
- a window!

LET'S GET STARTED

1

Gather together your materials. This project requires the different colours to be overlayed, so have a play around with different colour layering. Make a note of the combinations you like the most.

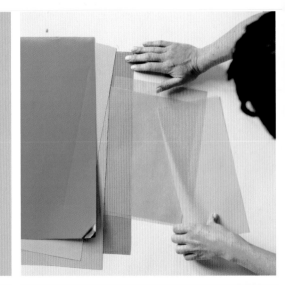

2

If you are using adhesive vinyl, you will need to peel back a corner to see how it will work with different colours.

3

Using the template, stanley knife and ruler, cut out the shapes in different colours on a cutting mat. If you are using adhesive vinyl, be aware that you will need to cut the oblong shapes in two different directions, as shown.

4

All the shapes work together to form a patchwork star design, but there are many different ways of doing this, especially when overlapping shapes. Here are some examples.

5

Start arranging the shapes to form patchwork stars on your window. It can take a minute to get your head around this, but once you have put together a few it will become easier.

OUT & ABOUT

I often list nature as
one of my main sources of
inspiration. Although nature and
animals are common themes in my work,
this is not neccessarily what I'm referring to
when I say nature inspires me. Being out in
the fresh air can change your perspective on
things. Sometimes if I am completely stuck
on a project, a change of scenery, particularly
an outdoors one, can do wonders. It refreshes
the eyes and opens up the mind, and that
kind of experience is invaluable when
trying to find inspiration.

With hyperactive kids and a small inner-city backyard, we spend a lot of time out and about. Of course, there are the obligatory trips to the park (which happen on almost a daily basis), but we are also spoilt with access to my mum's beach house and my dad's home in the country, so it's not hard to squeeze in adventures that are further afield.

When the budget permits, we also like overseas adventures. I always list travel as one of the best things to do, especially if you are a young designer looking to broaden your visual experience. I have been lucky enough to visit Japan almost every year for the past 10 years, and it has had a profound influence on my work. Tokyo is an obvious travel destination for anyone design-minded, and I find it gives me new ideas every time I visit. A friend once described Toyko as 'eyeball epilepsy' and it's totally true – from the packaging design to the shop displays, there is something amazing everywhere you look. But anywhere you visit can be inspiring. I recently returned from a family holiday to Malaysia with lots of ideas for new projects.

Travel doesn't need to be expensive or even have to mean travelling far. Despite us going to the expense of taking our kids overseas, their most favourite holiday was an Australian road trip where we hired a cheap little cabin in the mountains. It was the beginning of spring and still cold and raining, but we rugged up and went bushwalking, and saw lots of native animals. It's the one holiday they still regularly talk about.

Riding my bike is another outside activity that gives me inspiration. Cycling is one of the joys of my adult life. Not having my licence means I cycle everywhere around the city, and I often pick up ideas along the way. It's also functional and good for me, and yet still feels like total freedom.

And last but not least, when the weather is right, we like to eat outside as much as possible. Yes, we have favourite cafes that we like to frequent, but the most inspiring outdoor dining experiences are impromptu picnics. Living across the road from a park, this happens frequently when the weather is warm. And how could I not mention visits to Raph's food trucks? You can find us at any time of the year eating burgers or tacos in the park.

Whatever it is, being outside my house and studio is a vital part of the way my life fits together. Don't underestimate it!

GARDEN

I by no means have a green thumb, but I'm slowly learning. My current gardening skills tend to be quite haphazard – when I'm busy with work, my garden suffers, but spending time in the garden is something I am loving more and more each year. Plus, it's very satisfying – particularly growing your own food (I love having a little brag at the dinner table when something has come from the garden!). One day, when time permits, I can definitely see myself becoming an obsessive gardener.

My kids love gardening too, and I think it's important they learn where their food comes from. Ari always wants to dig and plant seeds, and gets so excited when the seedlings pop up, which is why I decided to make signs for our veggie patch. Ari is only four, and is yet to learn to read. When he goes out on a daily (sometimes hourly) basis to see what has grown, he always asks, "What did we plant there again?".

I made the veggie patch signs from wood and painted on letters and pictures so Ari could easily recognise each seedling. This meant I could also say, "Go and water the peas," and he would know which ones they were.

It also helped Tyke, who can read and whose vegetable knowledge is pretty good. But with the signs in place, I could send him out to the garden to pick certain things and know he would definitely be picking the right fruit or vegetable.

VEGGIE PATCH

After one winter in the garden, the signs work a treat (and look nice, too). I am currently creating new signs for our spring vegetable garden. Putting in this much effort really got me enthused about gardening.

BACKYARD

When I was a kid, we had a broken old swing set in our backyard. Although it lacked a swing, the frame provided the perfect place to make a cubby house. I remember spending hours with old sheets and blankets, creating the perfect outdoor hideaway. I also remember melting chocolate biscuits over candles in an effort to really recreate the camping experience. My mum wasn't too keen on that part.

Ari is perfect cubby-building age – for his last birthday we brought him a teepee, which is often stuffed with many toys and blankets to create the ultimate hideaway. He also loves to pile up every single cushion in our house on the lounge room floor to create a huge cushion house, or 'nest' as he refers to them. He is quite obsessive about them, and will get very upset if his 'nest' is disrupted. One day, sick of my lounge room being taken over by a cushion pile, I grabbed some sheets, blankets and rope and headed outside.

It only took me a few minutes to put this together, and when it was finished, I called the boys out to unveil the surprise.

They loved it, and spent the rest of the afternoon carting out more cushions and toys and snacks, and adding more ropes and adjusting it here and there.

CUBBY HOUSE

I loved it, too – not only did I get my lounge room back, but it reminded me just how easily (and cheaply) kids can be entertained with a simple idea and a little bit of creativity.

OP-SHOPS & MARKETS

Many of my most loved objects have come from op-shops and flea markets, so it's no surprise that this is one of my very favourite 'out and about' things to do. My mum was a keen op-shopper, and so my fascination with all things second hand started when I was quite young. When I reached my teens and I had little money for clothes, I frequently visited one of Melbourne's biggest and oldest trash and treasure markets. I'd make my way there early on a Sunday, and soon discovered how many great ideas and objects (and of course clothes) I could uncover.

Seeking out (or 'digging for', as I like to call it) something unique is a very personal process for me and one that I love. An object that one person has overlooked could be an absolute gem to you. To this day, waking up at the crack of dawn with the possibilities of treasures I might uncover at markets or venturing out to different suburbs to pick through op-shops still gives me the same amount of excitement as it did 20 years ago. And I don't think this will change any time soon!

PARK

Although I don't skateboard myself, it's a culture I have been immersed in from a young age. Raph ran a skateboard company when I met him, and I have worked for skateboard companies and designed skateboards myself.

We have always had decks lying around the house, and at the age of two Tyke got on a board and hasn't looked back since. Last Christmas, my dad made him a small wooden quarter pipe. It's stored in our garage and often gets wheeled out onto our wide footpath on weekends. Neighbourhood friends come and skate on it too – it's turned into quite a social thing to do!

Tyke decided that his quarter pipe looked a little boring, and asked if we could paint it. Having seen a few really awesome painted ramps, I was excited to do this. I redrew the ramp on my computer and sat down with the kids and we all sketched up some ideas.

After as much design discussion as a four-year-old and a nine-year-old can handle (15 minutes, if I'm lucky), we decided to paint some 'laser rays' and keep the rest of the design looking bold and geometric (and easy to paint!).

After quizzing a few painter friends, we decided the best paint to use was acrylic house paint. We went to our local hardware store, chose our colours and mixed up some sample pots. We painted the ramp with a white undercoat first.

Tyke was a keen volunteer painter! Because we had to let the paint dry in the different sections, the ramp took a few sessions to complete, which actually worked well with my kids' short attention spans.

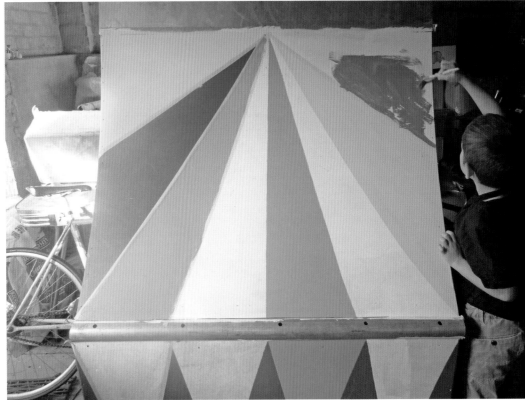

SKATEBOARD

As soon as the ramp was dry, we took it out for a test run. Tyke said that the paint made the ramp more 'slippery', but he was genuinely pleased with how it turned out. Even Raph, the skateboard purist, was impressed.

OUT
& ABOUT
PROJECTS

As you can see, spending time 'out and about' is something we do quite a lot, and it's a really important part of my life in general. Even though you might not think it's directly related to what I do, being outdoors is actually a very integral part of my design process. Here are some projects that will hopefully inspire you to get out and about, too!

RECYCLED PLANTERS

{ DIFFICULTY: easy }

We are blessed with a neighbourhood that has a lot of great Mediterranean and Middle Eastern grocery stores. It's a big part of why we originally chose to live in the suburb we do. On my first shopping adventure in our new hood, I bought tins of things not knowing what was inside, simply for the beauty of the graphics on the outside.

We have now tried most of the things in the tins, resulting in us finding some new favourite foods – and some things we are still not sure what they are. But I've also found a new use for the tins with pretty graphics, many of which I could not bring myself to throw out: turning them into planters for my garden (they also make great storage tins for pencils or cutlery).

YOU WILL NEED

- empty tins – ones with labels printed on the tin work best
- tin opener
- screwdriver and hammer
- potting mix
- seedlings

1

Carefully remove the lids off the tins with a tin opener.

2

Make sure the lid comes off clean. Add some drainage holes in the bottom of the tin by gently hammering a screwdriver into it.

3

Add some potting mix to the bottom of the tin, then remove seedlings from their packets and place in the tin with the potting mix. Add enough potting mix to fill up the tin.

4

Gently push the seedlings down so they are firmly in the tin. The deeper the tin, the more room there will be for the roots to grow. Use smaller tins for seedlings if you plan to re-pot them. Water the seedlings thoroughly.

5

Place your recycled planters on windowsills or outside (although they will rust outside – but that's kind of nice, too).

BEADED POT PLANT HOLDER

{ DIFFICULTY: hard }

In my experience, you can never have enough indoor plants. My lounge currently looks like a veritable jungle, and everyone in my family likes it a lot.

Apparently, indoor plants improve air quality and your mental health, too. As I am prone to spending way too much time in front of my computer, I'm often in need of both of these things. But overall, I like indoor plants simply because they look lovely.

Here is a pot hanger you can make yourself – it looks tricky, but if you can tie a basic knot, you can make it. I searched everywhere for large wooden beads and eventually bought some online. You can even make your own coloured beads using modelling clay. I used a woven cotton cord for the rope – I have gone for a neutral look here, but rope is available in lots of great colours – go crazy!

YOU WILL NEED

- white paint pen
- Eight 40 mm (1.5 in) natural wooden beads
- 5 metres (16 ft 8 in) of sturdy rope or cord
- masking tape (cute pattern optional)
- Four 40 mm (1.5 in) white wooden beads
- potted plant

LET'S GET STARTED

1

Add patterns to your natural beads with the white paint pen. I painted four beads with stripes and four with small dots. Leave to dry.

2

Cut your rope or cord into eight even lengths. Seal the ends of the rope with tape – this will prevent fraying and make bead-threading easier. Knot all the rope lengths together approximately 10–15 cm (4–6 in) from the bottom.

3

Divide the rope lengths into pairs and knot each of them at an even length approximately 15 cm (6 in) from the first knot.

4

Divide the ropes again into new pairs by taking two ropes that sit next to each other (but have not already been knotted together) and knotting them together at an even length of approximately 20 cm (8 in) from the previous knots.

192 Find & Keep

5

Add the beads. String three of each onto each pair of ropes. I added one natural bead, followed by one white, followed by a final natural bead.

6

Once all the beads are threaded onto the ropes, tie a knot at the ends to secure the beads in place.

7

Tie all the ropes into a final single knot at the top. Make sure this knot is super-tight, as this is the knot the plant will hang from.

Now place the pot plant inside the holder – it will sit on top of the first knot you tied.

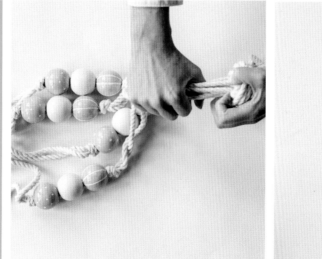

KITE

{ DIFFICULTY: hard }

Since we live across the road from a park, kite flying is something we enjoy on a regular basis. There is nothing quite like sitting on the grass at the start of spring, flying a kite in a gentle breeze. It's one of those simple pleasures that can't help but be relaxing. As with many things, I also think kites make super-nice wall decorations, especially in kids' rooms.

This project shows you how to make your own classic diamond-shaped kite. Technically, it should fly, but it's probably better suited as a wall decoration. You can, of course, try and fly it if you feel inspired – just make sure the breeze is really gentle.

For the kite body I used handmade paper from my local art store. It seemed a bit more sturdy than tissue paper, but still very light.

YOU WILL NEED

- stanley knife
- 2 thin wooden rods
- masking tape
- 3 metres (10 ft) string
- paper for kite body
- tissue paper for decorating
- paper streamers for decorating
- paper glue

LET'S GET STARTED

1

Using a stanley knife, cut your wooden rods down so that one is about three-quarters the size of the other. This will form the kite structure.

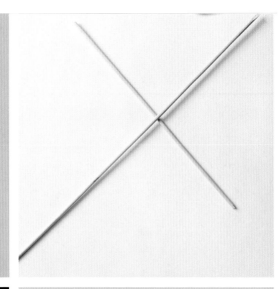

2

Attach the wooden pieces together by winding around some masking tape. The pieces should sit perpendicular to each other, with the shorter rod sitting horizontally.

3

Add notches to the ends of the wooden rods – just big enough to hold the string in place.

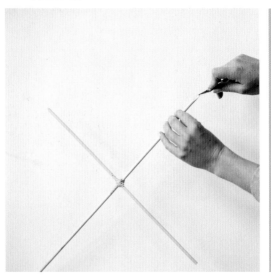

4

Starting at one corner, lace the string around the edge of the wooden frame, using the notches to hold the string in place. Pull it quite taut and knot it once you have returned to your starting point.

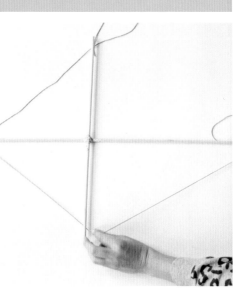

5

Secure the string with tape at each corner of the frame.

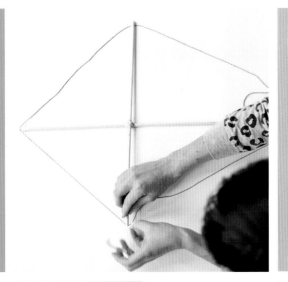

6

Cut your kite paper to the size of the frame, leaving a border of 5–7cm (2–2½ in).

7

Fold the extra paper over the string and tape securely into place the whole way around.

8

Decorate the front of the kite – I used tissue paper cut into geometric shapes. Finish your kite by adding a tail to the bottom of the frame using paper streamers.

Tip

If you do intend to fly the kite, don't forget to add a string from the corners of the horizontal rod so you have something to hold on to. Happy flying!

PICNIC CUTLERY SET

{ DIFFICULTY: easy }

So, you have a picnic coming up and you want to add some details to make it extra special – well, this project will do the trick. And I know what you are thinking – who has the time to make disposable cutlery look good? Believe it or not, YOU DO! This project is maximum impact but minimum time, and the results are so good. So good, in fact, that you won't be disposing of this cutlery any time soon. And don't think they are just for kids' parties – grown-ups will love these details too (well, grown-ups with fine taste will, anyway!).

Some of these techniques are quicker than others, so if you are really stretched for time, just go with adding stickers or pretty tape. You can pick up wooden cutlery sets from party supply stores or online.

YOU WILL NEED

- wooden cutlery
- plain colour stickers in a variety of colours and shapes
- patterned washi tape
- acrylic paint
- paintbrushes

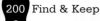

1

Assemble all your materials and separate them into different piles.

2

Start to apply your stickers to the cutlery. Here, I have simply wrapped circle stickers around each handle to create a scallop effect, but you can also try placing different-coloured circles in a straight row, a polka dot design or placing different-sized dots together.

3

For the knives I have used stripes of different-patterned tape, but you can also tape up the whole handle or add diagonal stripes.

 Using square or triangle stickers, I have cut down smaller triangles and added them to the edges of the fork handles. You can also try cutting out diamonds in different colours, pointing different-coloured triangles in opposite directions or using stripes in varying widths and colours.

5 You can also mask off areas to create straight lines with paint. Add the tape to the area you do not want to paint, paint the unmasked area and a small piece of the tape to create a straight edge. Once the paint is dry, remove the tape. Combine the painted area with any of the above mediums.

DRIFTWOOD WIND CHIME

{ DIFFICULTY: easy }

I wouldn't exactly call our family beach-bums, but in summer, thanks to my mum's beach house, we do manage quite a bit of beach time. Our kids always go foraging for different bits and pieces, and every trip they return from the beach with a bag of shells, a bucket of seaweed and jellyfish, or possibly even part of a decapitated seagull.

Driftwood is something that also often makes it back to our place. Yes, it can look nice just as decoration, but there is only so much driftwood one can fit on the mantelpiece. So here is a beachy holiday-type project that puts spare driftwood to good use. Hang it in the breeze and let it tinkle away – you will feel like you're back by the ocean before you know it.

If you don't live close to a beach, any smooth regular sticks will do.

YOU WILL NEED

- driftwood
- acrylic paint
- paintbrush
- approximately 2 metres (6 ft 7 in) different-coloured synthetic string

LET'S GET STARTED

1

Select your pieces of driftwood. Look for one longer piece to tie the other pieces to. Also look for different widths and lengths so they make different sounds when they bump together. Even test how they sound by knocking them together.

2

Paint your driftwood pieces. I wanted to keep the wood looking as natural as possible, so I used minimal decoration. You can use the masking tape technique on page 203 to help you achieve straight lines.

3

Once your driftwood is dry, fasten string around the top of each piece with a knot, and then bind and tie it again to secure it.

I used lengths of string approximately 45 cm (18 in) long, but you can play around with different lengths to suit your wind chime.

4

Tie each piece of string to the long piece of driftwood you've reserved for the top of your wind chime. Tie the string at regular intervals.

5

Add a 60 cm (24 in) piece of string to the longest piece of driftwood. Bind the piece of string at each end to make a handle. Hang from anywhere that catches a breeze.

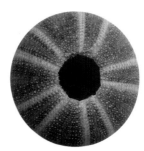

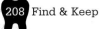

EASY PICNIC TREATS

{ DIFFICULTY: easy }

We obsess over food quite a lot in our house. Cookbooks are scoured, ingredients are hunted down, and many, many recipes are tested. It sort of comes with the territory when you have a partner in the food business. While I'm absolutely not complaining, I also believe food doesn't have to be complicated to be delicious. Quite the contrary, actually.

Here are three of my favourite recipes, all perfect for a picnic and all simple to put together. Use the freshest and very best ingredients you can afford – I always try to go for organic and local whenever possible – this will result in maximum deliciousness.

1

Beci's favourite sandwich

1 fresh baguette
2 tomatoes
sea salt and freshly cracked
    black pepper
1 ball fior de latte cheese
small handful basil leaves
good quality extra-virgin olive oil

Cut the baguette into three pieces.
Slice the tomato and season with
salt and pepper. Slice the cheese.
Slice open each baguette piece and
add the tomato and fior de latte,
then top with basil leaves. Drizzle
with olive oil and serve.

Serves 3

2

Limeade

275 g (10 oz/1¼ cups) sugar
1 tablespoon grated lime zest
375 ml (12 fl oz/1½ cups) fresh
    lime juice
fresh mint, to serve

Tip

If you would like to make different-flavoured drinks, use lemons, oranges or pink grapefruit, or your own combination. You can adjust the amount of sugar used to suit your taste.

In a medium saucepan, bring 125 ml (4 fl oz/½ cup) water to the boil. Add the sugar and grated lime zest, and stir until the sugar has dissolved. Remove from the heat and set aside to cool. Stir in the lime juice and 1½ litres (51 fl oz/7 cups) iced water. Add the fresh mint just before serving.

Serves 6

3

Salted caramel popcorn

60 g (2 oz/⅓ cup) brown sugar
1 large tablespoon golden syrup
1 large tablespoon butter
1 teaspoon vanilla extract
1 teaspoon water
60 g (2 oz/¼ cup) unpopped popcorn
sea salt, to taste

Stir all the ingredients except the popcorn and salt together in a small saucepan over low heat, until the sugar is dissolved and the butter has melted. Increase the heat and bring to the boil for a few minutes. Remove from the heat and set aside. Cook the popcorn according to packet instructions. Pour the caramel sauce over the popped corn, sprinkle with sea salt and mix well. This recipe multiplies easily.

Serves 3

SUCCULENT GARDEN

{ DIFFICULTY: easy }

Succulents and cacti suit my gardening style – that is, I very much like gardening, but my current work/family/life situation means that gardening comes at the bottom of my caring-for-living-things list. Succulents understand this predicament and are quite forgiving of it. They might shrivel up a little without love and water, but survive pretty well with the moments of attention I am able to give them.

I also like how easy they are to propagate. I may or may not have snuck out after dark on a few occasions to snip off succulent cuttings from neighbouring gardens. I'm not saying any more about that, especially as you could be my neighbour!

Here is my version of putting those cuttings and other collected succulents to good use.

YOU WILL NEED

- variety of succulents and/or cacti plants
- large metal planter approximately 35 cm (14 in) wide x 27 cm (11 in) long x 16 cm (6 in) deep
- stones or pebbles for drainage in the planter and also for placing on top
- succulent potting mix

LET'S GET STARTED

1

Choose a variety of succulents and cacti. Try to choose plants of different colours, heights, widths, shapes and textures.

2

With the plants still in their pots, play around with plant composition until you are happy with the look of your succulent garden.

3

Here, I have chosen to put the biggest ones at the back and have tried to separate any plants that are similar. I have also placed a plant that will grow over the edge on the side of the planter.

4

Remove all the plants, remembering where you placed them, and add some rocks to the bottom of the planter – this will aid drainage (succulents and cacti hate soggy soil). Add some potting mix to the bottom of the planter.

5

Remove the plants from their pots and put in position. Add more potting mix around the plants until the planter is full. Press the plants down firmly (but gently) into the potting mix.

6

Add some stones to the top of the garden and around the plants. This not only looks nice, but again aids with drainage of the soil.

BIKE BASKET

{ DIFFICULTY: easy }

Being a non-driver, riding my bike is something I do quite often. Yes, I do love it, but it's also a functional way of running errands around my neighbourhood. I even have one of those little bike trailers which Ari sits in, comfortably carrying him and my shopping and anything else I can fit in, too. Every time I take it out I'm pretty sure I inadvertently wear a smug 'I'm-greener-than-you' grin (sorry if you've had to experience that).

The trailer can be a bit cumbersome for just a quick trip down to the shops, which is where this handy basket comes in. I can't take credit for the genius idea of using pet collars to attach the basket to the bike. This idea came from a guy at my local bike shop – thanks Hugh!

It's best to use a basket with a flat side so that it will sit nicely on the front of your bike.

YOU WILL NEED

- basket
- scissors or stanley knife
- paint
- paintbrushes
- 2 small pet collars

LET'S GET STARTED

1

Check out your basket, to see which parts (if any) you will need to remove, and how easily removable these parts will be.

2

Remove any unnecessary basket parts. Here, I am detaching the bottle holders. They were held on with leather straps that were easily cut through with scissors.

3

To remove the handle I used a stanley knife and cut through the parts of the wicker that were holding it onto the main part of the basket. After a bit of manoeuvring and select cutting, the handle came away easily.

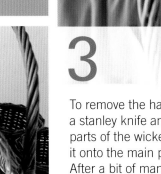

4

Paint your basket. I chose three different colours and painted random parts of the basket, as I didn't want to lose the quality of the natural wicker colour.

5

Attach the basket to the handlebars with the pet collars.

Tip
Try to space the collars at an even distance, and attach them firmly to prevent your basket contents from going everywhere when you are riding!

TEMPLATES

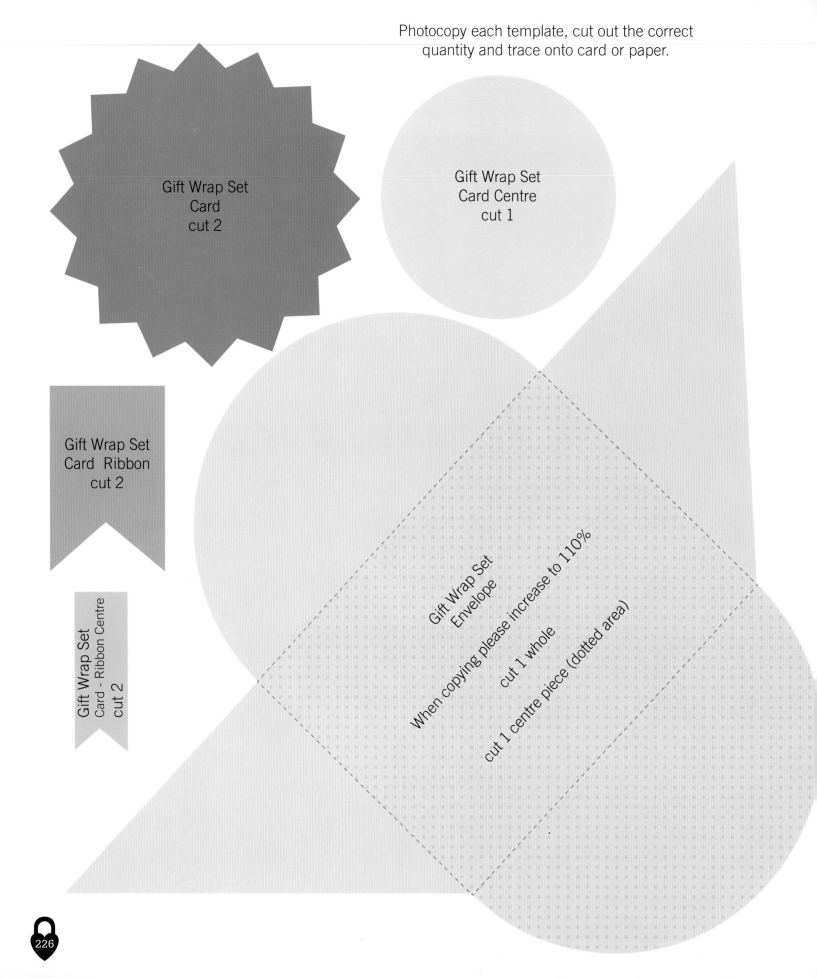

Photocopy each template, cut out the correct quantity and trace onto card or paper.

Gift Wrap Set
Card
cut 2

Gift Wrap Set
Card Centre
cut 1

Gift Wrap Set
Card Ribbon
cut 2

Gift Wrap Set
Card - Ribbon Centre
cut 2

Gift Wrap Set
Envelope

When copying please increase to 110%

cut 1 whole

cut 1 centre piece (dotted area)

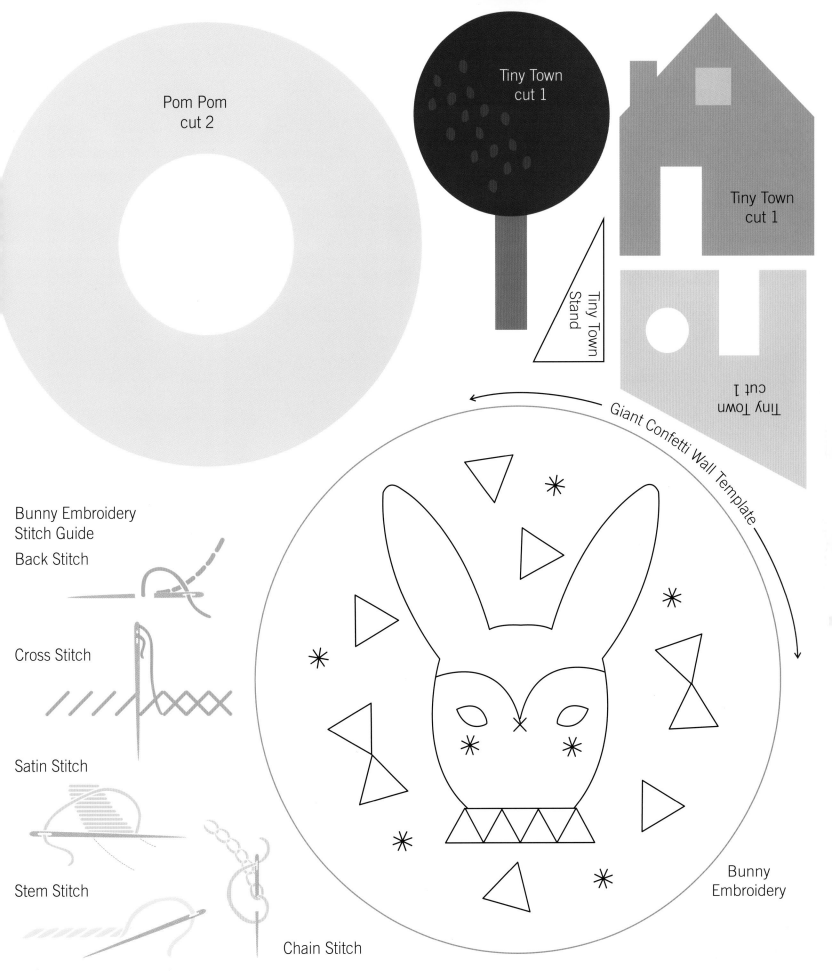

Pom Pom
cut 2

Tiny Town
cut 1

Tiny Town
cut 1

Tiny Town
cut 1

Tiny Town
Stand

Giant Confetti Wall Template

Bunny Embroidery
Stitch Guide

Back Stitch

Cross Stitch

Satin Stitch

Stem Stitch

Chain Stitch

Bunny
Embroidery

Tiny Town
cut 1 each

Cake Stencil

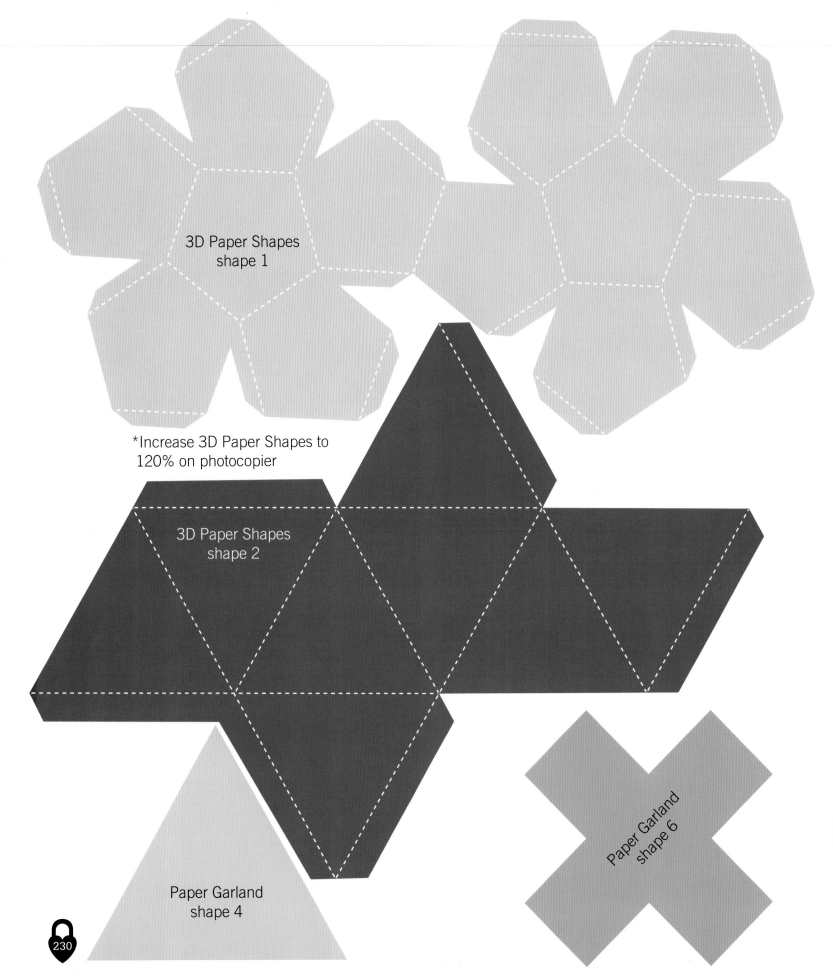

3D Paper Shapes
shape 1

*Increase 3D Paper Shapes to
120% on photocopier

3D Paper Shapes
shape 2

Paper Garland
shape 4

Paper Garland
shape 6

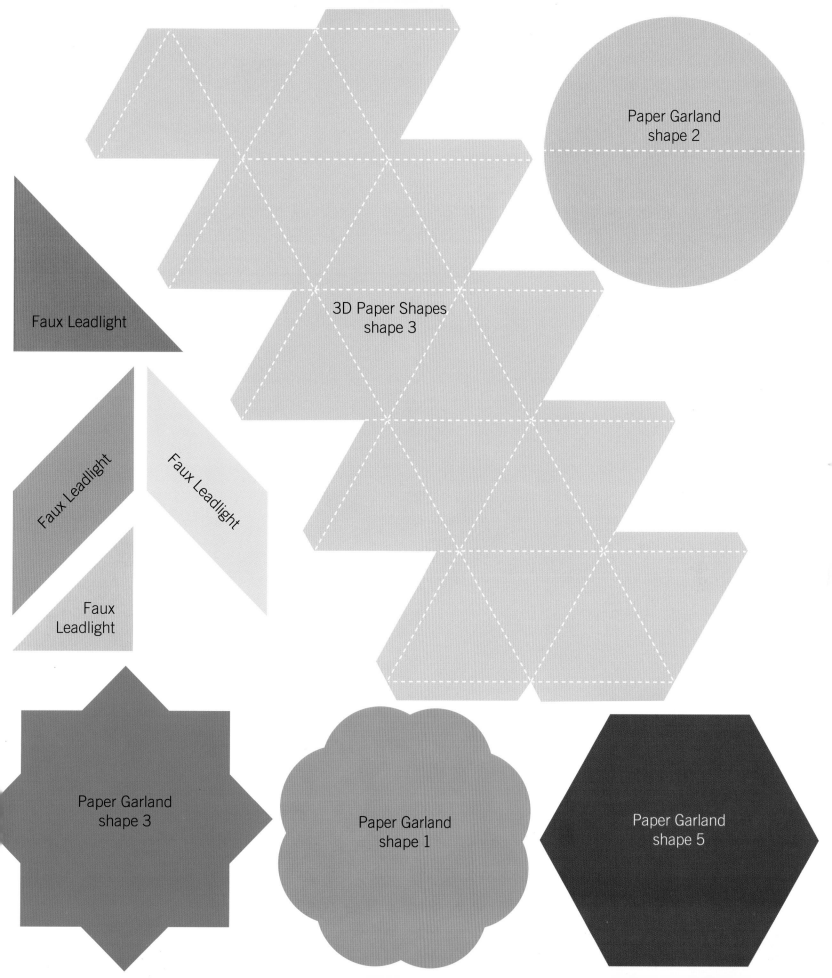

Faux Leadlight

Paper Garland
shape 2

3D Paper Shapes
shape 3

Faux Leadlight

Faux Leadlight

Faux
Leadlight

Paper Garland
shape 3

Paper Garland
shape 1

Paper Garland
shape 5

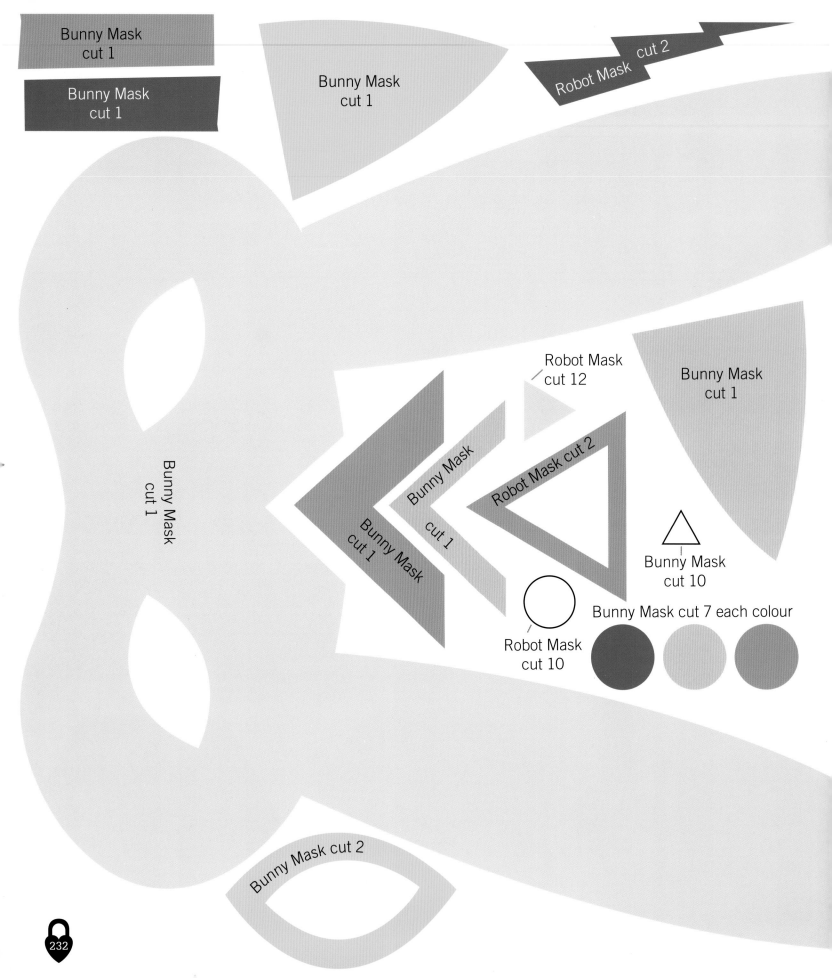

Bunny Mask
cut 1

Bunny Mask
cut 1

Bunny Mask
cut 1

Robot Mask cut 2

Bunny Mask
cut 1

Robot Mask
cut 12

Bunny Mask
cut 1

Bunny Mask
cut 1

Bunny Mask
cut 1

Robot Mask cut 2

Bunny Mask
cut 10

Robot Mask
cut 10

Bunny Mask cut 7 each colour

Bunny Mask cut 2

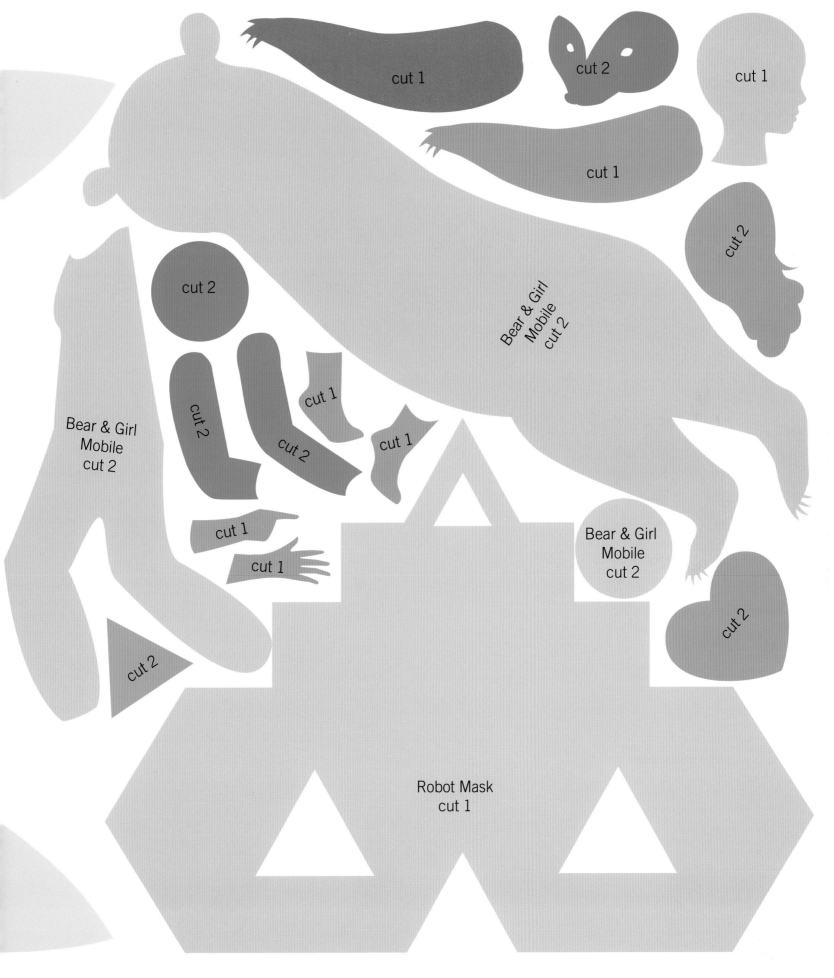

cut 1

cut 2

cut 1

cut 1

cut 2

cut 2

Bear & Girl
Mobile
cut 2

cut 2

cut 1

cut 2

Bear & Girl
Mobile
cut 2

cut 1

cut 1

Bear & Girl
Mobile
cut 2

cut 2

cut 2

Robot Mask
cut 1

THANK YOU

Thank you to:

My family: Raph – my sounding board, chauffeur, personal chef, babysitter, C.A.T. team, business manager, best friend and numero uno everything; Tyke and Ari – you both amaze me every day with your awesomeness; and of course Dad, Mum, Erwin, Emily, Sean, Leslie, Rudin, Brooke, Zeddy, Joh, Andie, Julie, Annie and Norm.

Tio and Miso: for keeping me company in the wee hours.

The people who have helped me along my way: Paul Jones (my high-school graphics teacher), Rei Zunde, Patrick Snelling, Andrea McNamara, Meredith Rowe, Georgia Chapman, Shauna Toohey, Misha Hollenbach, Camillo and Monica Ipolliti, Phil Ivanov, Masami Asai, Elska Sandor, Catherine Lyons, Wendy Mullin, Maurice Menares, *Monster Children* magazine, Chanie Stock, Martin Mackintosh, Gemma Jones, *Relax* magazine, Rebecca Wolkenstien, Lisa Gorman, Jo Walker, Lara Burke, *Frankie* magazine, Sonia Le, Justine Clarke, Lucy Feagins, Shinjiro Nishino, Risa Nakazawa, Abi Crompton, David Lopes, Dan Rule, Megan Morton, Lawrence Greenwood, Harvest Textiles, and Rae Ganim. I'm sure I've forgotten some peeps but if you ever gave me a step-up or an opportunity – I whole-heartedly thank you.

The folks at Hardie Grant: in particular Paul McNally – for giving me the opportunity to do this book, and Lucy Heaver – for putting up with my very non-editor ways of working.

Michelle Mackintosh: book designer extraordinaire, British shorthair expert and all-round amazing person. Also thanks to Steve Wide and Bronte for making me feel so welcome.

Chris Middleton: for being the most patient and calm photographer/person I have ever met.

Kirra Jamison and Sue DeGennaro: extra-special thanks for your ears and eyes and advice during this process.

My amazing and talented group of friends: Misha, Shauna and Odi; Ed, Olivia, Sofia and Milo; Conor, Amanda and Bonnie; Kirra and Dane; Max and Rosie; Bridget and Micheal; Fawn and Jeff; Masami, Goro, Mei and Teppei; Bonnie.M; Sally and Micah; Chris Midds; Leah and Tim; Luke and Lauren; Nat and Frank; Tristan and Age; Pip; Lisa and Josh; Daniela; Brendan Huntley; Danny Young; BT and Di, Nat, Matt and Lily; Fryman; Sebo and Lou, Sheena (best and hottest babysitter ever); Sarah FP.

Jeremy Worstman and the Jacky Winter crew: you are the game-changers!

My freelance clients: for being so patient in general, and especially while I was working on this book.

My studio helpers: Kristina Sabarosedin and Natalie Turnbull; Sam Morgan for being a web genius.

The universe: for allowing me to do something I truly love for a job.

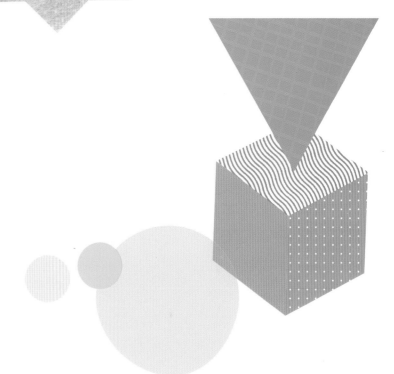

Published in 2012 by Hardie Grant Books

Hardie Grant Books (Australia)
Ground Floor, Building 1,
658 Church Street
Richmond, Victoria 3121
www.hardiegrant.com.au

Hardie Grant Books (UK)
North Suite, Dudley House
Southampton Street
London WC2E 7HF
www.hardiegrant.co.uk

A Cataloguing-in-Publication entry is available from the catalogue of the National Library of Australia at www.nla.gov.au

Publishing Director: Paul McNally
Managing Editor: Lucy Heaver
Project Text Editor: Anna Goode
Design Manager: Heather Menzies
Designer: Michelle Mackintosh
Photographer: Chris Middleton
Production Manager: Todd Rechner
Production Assistant: Sarah Trotter

Colour reproduction by Splitting Image Colour Studio
Printed in China by 1010 Printing International Limited

The publisher and Beci would like to thank After, Gorman, Greg Hatton, Loom Rugs, Mr Kitly, Scout House, Sticky Fingers Bakery, The Junk Company, Third Drawer Down, Tractor Home, Tokyo Bike for their generosity in supplying props for this book.

The publisher and Beci would like to thank Valentine gifts of MITSUKOSHI ISETAN, by Goncharoff and Gas As Interface Co. Ltd for permission to reuse photographs in this book.

The publisher and Beci would like to thank helpers at the photoshoot: Catie Maher, Natalie Turnbull, Amy Mcgown, Meredith Forrester, Amelia Letuzzi, Ella Schwatz and Tina Thompson.

Additional photographs supplied by Beci Orpin, Raph Rashid, Kirra Jamison, Koshi Haneishi and Masayoshi Taki.

Additional scanning by Karl Stamer at Lantern Printing.

Models: Pia Cattapan, courtesy of Priscilla's; Odette, Tyke and Ari.

Every effort has been made to incorporate correct information. The publishers regret any errors or omissions and invite readers to contribute up-to-date information to Hardie Grant Books.